AFTER THE MERGER

REVISED EDITION

AFTER THE MERGER

The Authoritative Guide for Integration Success

PRICE PRITCHETT
with DONALD ROBINSON and RUSSELL CLARKSON
Pritchett and Associates, Inc.
Dallas, Texas

McGraw-Hill

New York ◆ San Francisco ◆ Washington, D.C. ◆ Auckland
Bogotá ◆ Caracas ◆ Lisbon ◆ London ◆ Madrid ◆ Mexico City
Milan ◆ Montreal ◆ New Delhi ◆ San Juan ◆ Singapore
Sydney ◆ Tokyo ◆ Toronto

Library of Congress Cataloging-in-Publication Data

Pritchett, Price.
    After the merger : the authoritative guide for integration success
    Price Pritchett, with Donald Robinson and Russell Clarkson. — 2nd ed.
      p.   cm.
    Includes index.
    ISBN 0-7863-1239-4
    1. Consolidation and merger of corporations.   I. Robinson, Donald.
    II. Clarkson, Russell.
    HD2746.5.P74 1997
    658. 1 ' 6—dc21   97–13951
                                                             CIP

McGraw-Hill

*A Division of The **McGraw·Hill** Companies*

7 8 9 0 DOC/DOC 9 0 2 1 0 9

ISBN 0-7863-1239-4

The sponsoring editor for this book was Steven Sheehan, the editing supervisor was Donna Namorato, and the production supervisor was Suzanne W. B. Rapcavage. It was set in Palatino by Carol Graphics.

Printed and bound by R.R. Donnelley & Sons Company.

This publication is designed to provide accurate and authoritative information in regard to the subject matter covered. It is sold with the understanding that neither the author or the publisher is engaged in rendering legal, accounting, or other professional service. If legal advice or other expert assistance is required, the services of a competent professional person should be sought.

    —From a Declaration of Principles jointly adopted by a committee
    of the American Bar Association and a Committee of Publishers.

McGraw-Hill books are available at special quantity discounts to use as premiums and sales promotions, or for use in corporate training programs. For more information, please write to the Director of Special Sales, McGraw-Hill, 11 West 19th Street, New York, NY 10011. Or contact your local bookstore.

 This book is printed on recycled, acid-free paper containing a minimum of 50% recycled de-inked fiber.

CONTENTS

PART TWO

RESOLVING REDUNDANCIES AND STAFFING ISSUES

After the Merger was the first book ever published on merger-integration strategy. Library Journal named it "one of the ten best business books of the year" in 1985. It has remained in print and enjoyed steady sales for over a decade now, evidence that the book's insights and advice are sound enough to endure the test of time.

But the merger scene has changed dramatically during the past decade or so. For one thing, today's deals are quite different. For another, the pace of change in general has accelerated, and this puts more concurrent pressures on companies seeking to acquire and merge.

What hasn't changed much over the years, however, is the hit rate on merger success. Deal traffic recently hit an all-time high. But, overall, companies don't seem to be doing any better job at merger management than they did a decade ago. Studies continue to find that, on the whole, well over half of all acquisitions fail to earn back the cost of capital.

Some mergers and acquisitions, of course, are poorly conceived and offer little hope from the beginning. But the biggest reason behind the high failure rate is badly flawed integration management. In some cases, the merger-integration strategy itself is all wrong. In other situations, the game plan for merging is good enough, but foul-ups in execution cripple the chances for success.

This revised edition of After the Merger tells managers and executives how to beat the odds. With another decade of merger consulting experience to draw upon, we offer new management insights along with enhancements to our integration methodology. As the years have passed, our work with a wide variety of merger clients has given us an ever-growing appreciation of the need for speed, for discipline in transition management, and for counterintuitive moves.

From our perspective, mergers remain the ultimate change challenge. But they also provide a unique opportunity to energize an organization, create a more change-adaptive culture, and achieve unconventional growth. This revised edition of *After the Merger* offers coaching on how to reach those worthy objectives.

Mergers and acquisitions serve as one form of corporate growth, and it's worth remembering that growth, whether in an individual or an organization, frequently brings with it some discomfort as well as some awkward behavior. How can executives and managers best handle these growing pains? What can be done to overcome the adolescent clumsiness that comes from newly developed corporate muscle not yet matched by coordination?

The best steps probably are preventive ones. But because of the nature of acquisitions—how the deals are pursued, negotiated, and finally struck—many problems cannot be preempted. They can only be anticipated, met head-on, and dealt with in a professional and timely manner.

Certainly one of the things top management can do is be prepared for the organizational dissonance that is virtually always one of the upshots of merger/acquisition activity. The destabilizing force that is generated opens the door for change, for positive effect. It is a motivating force top management can seize to fuel growth and improve performance. It is energy that can be harnessed.

The dissonance must be managed intelligently and carefully channeled, or it can be disastrous. The upheaval is not something to be stifled, sidestepped, or ignored. It should be parlayed into a positive thrust. But only rarely is it fully exploited for its potential benefit to both firms involved.

Often the dissonance—the psychological shock waves—appear to be unexpected, poorly understood, and inadequately governed. As a result, there is much organizational trauma that could have been avoided, and many potential benefits of the destablization are not seized.

The people responsible for engineering mergers and acquisitions have developed a high degree of expertise in handling the legal and financial aspects of the deal. Regrettably, there is no corresponding sophistication in postmerger management. And regardless of how astute a job the deal makers do, the merger is not going be a bargain if management doesn't make it work.

So this is a book about managing, rather than making, mergers and acquisitions. The intent is to sharpen managerial insight and understanding into the unique dynamics that characterize this form of corporate development. It is an effort to give direction and straightforward answers to executives and managers who must carry the burden of making the merger measure up to the potential the deal makers originally conceived.

Every year, thousands of acquisitions must be shepherded by new owners and managers. These people need guidelines, plus a frame of reference that makes sense of the problems peculiar to this organizational event.

The symptomatology and underlying problems are remarkably consistent, regardless of the size of the companies being acquired. It may be a megadeal, such as Boeing buying McDonnell Douglas or Hilton attempting a takeover of ITT Sheraton. It may be a foreign acquirer such as British Telecommunications purchasing MCI to get a foothold in the U.S. market. Finally, there are innumerable owner/entrepreneurs who take their life savings and commit to a scary load of personal debt to buy some little business that another individual started but now wants to sell.

Granted, every single merger agreement that is reached will be unique in some respects. But there will be a remarkable number of features they all hold in common—enough that managers and executives can be told what to expect and how to contend with the situation most effectively.

That is the purpose of this book.

PART ONE

Understanding the Dynamics of Mergers and Acquisitions

CHAPTER 1

Problems in Buying a "Used" Company

It is lunchtime on a Thursday at the University Club in downtown Chicago. The three businessmen seated at a table near the window are on their last cup of coffee. One is the CEO of an acquisition-minded pharmaceutical company. Another is the president of a major insurance company that recently bought a financial service firm. The third owns a small manufacturing company, and he is in the process of selling his firm. The lunch crowd is thinning out, but at this table the conversation isn't lagging.

The pharmaceutical executive leans into the table, eyes the other two, and growls, "It's a helluva lot like buying a second-hand car. We try to do our homework, but the preacquisition analyses never tell us all we need to know about how the outfit has been run. It's like kicking the tires, looking under the hood, and driving the car around the block. You're probably going to have a tough time seeing things the seller doesn't want you to see. Negotiations are the same whether you're buying a car or a company. That other guy is going to highlight the positives while concealing or downplaying problems. Every company we've bought since I became CEO has given us some nasty surprises."

Nodding and looking out the window across the Chicago skyline, the insurance company president adds, "We're facing the same problems right now with a company we just acquired. We're beginning to realize that the previous owner drove the car differently. When he owned the company, it was one-man rule. But we operate in a decentralized fashion, so it's like the whole family has to know how to drive. The previous owner also pampered the machine, while our management style and philosophy is to drive hard. We're beginning to wonder if the acquisition will be able to handle the strain. On top of these problems, we have to deal with the negative press coverage we've been getting from the business journals. They keep writing that we're not knowledgeable about how to operate this kind of vehicle, that we don't have anybody who knows how to drive it. Where we really ran into problems was when we lost some of the seasoned executives we had expected would stay at the wheel, guys that had an outstanding track record."

The owner of the manufacturing firm grins at his two companions and says, "So I'm supposed to have something in common with the used car salesman? Well, let me play with that for a minute. Sure, I'm selling an organization that needs some repairs. I doubt that the people who are buying me out really know how well my company has been maintained. Furthermore, I don't know if they are mentally or financially prepared to make the repairs or, in other words, to give the organization what it needs."

"They plan on doing a minor tune-up, while you're sitting here knowing it's really due for a major overhaul, right?" the insurance company president says.

The owner/entrepreneur squints back at the insurance company president and replies, "That's probably being a little too hard on me. Besides, I get the feeling they're planning on dismantling the car and selling off some of the parts anyhow."

The CEO reflects on this for a few moments, then asks, "What happens to the whole when they sell off some of the parts? Is there going to be a breakdown? We tried that approach two years ago, and I guess we must have inadvertently sold the wheels because that acquisition never went anywhere."

"Well, it's basically out of my hands," the manufacturing executive says. "There's a lot I could have told the guys who are buying me out, but they never asked the right questions. In fact, they haven't paid much attention to what I did tell them. The word I get from my old employees who are still with the company is that nobody's listening to them either. So what the hell? God helps those who help themselves."

As the three men get up from the table to leave, the president of the insurance company remarks, "I guess so. But whoever said 'What you don't know can't hurt you' obviously didn't know beans about mergers and acquisitions."

STATISTICS ON MERGER SUCCESS AND FAILURE

Nobody has a very precise set of statistics regarding the success rate for mergers and acquisitions in the United States. One key reason is that, according to the Federal Trade Commission (FTC), approximately 60 percent of all merger activity is never publicized or consists of small transactions (less than million-dollar deals) that no one tracks systematically. According to the studies that have been conducted and the merger monitoring that is reported, though, growth through acquisition is a risky business.

Available statistics generally indicate that, on the whole, acquirers have less than a 50-50 chance of being successful in merger/acquisition ventures.

Granted, success is a qualitative issue. What looks like success today may subsequently turn out to be a fiasco. And current disappointments can sometimes blossom forth to become outstanding moneymakers. But the grim facts remain—far too many mergers go bad.

Over a decade ago, Acquisition Horizons studied data on 537 companies that had made at least one acquisition within a five-year time frame. Over 40 percent of the respondents described their acquisition efforts as only *somewhat successful* or *unsuccessful*. The most frequently mentioned reason for the disappointing results was that management in the acquired firm was not as strong as expected. Other major reasons were that the preacquisition research proved inadequate or inaccurate, the systems were not as well-developed as had been thought, a new strategic plan was needed for the acquired firm, integration planning was not all that it should have been, and finally, some of the key management talent left the firm. The companies studied ranged in size from $125 million to over $2 billion in annual sales.

Another 1980s study conducted by *Fortune* magazine analyzed 10 major conglomerate acquisitions made during 1971.[1] All acquisitions represented a move by the parent company into a new line of business, and the question posed by the study was, "Do conglomerate mergers make sense?" At least at the end of the 10-year period when this backward look occurred, they did not.

Michael Porter made an even longer-term measurement, studying the success rate of 33 highly regarded companies over a 36-year period of acquiring. His data revealed that over half of the "unrelated" acquisitions were later divested.

Research by McKinsey & Company found a failure rate of 61 percent in acquisition programs, with failure defined as not earning a sufficient return (cost of capital) on the funds invested. Considering how much hard work and emotional strain are involved in managing mergers and acquisitions, it seems appropriate to say, so much effort . . . so little return.

The obvious question is "What's going wrong? Why do the statistics look so bad?" Undoubtedly, all acquirers are well-intentioned in their growth plans and fully expect to be successful in the buying and blending of other firms. Some of the failures and disappointments can be legitimately explained away, attributed to something like an unfavorable economic turn of events. Sometimes the acquisition was a mismatch in the first place, with small odds for success. A high percentage of merger difficulties and failures, though, derives directly from faulty management. Target companies are strategically sought and strategically stalked, but then the follow-up acts are poorly orchestrated. The acquirer stumbles along, improvising instead of following a strategically designed, systematically conducted program for corporate integration. Hard to believe, with this much money at stake? A study by the Boston Consulting Group found that, prior to the acquisition, fewer than 20 percent of companies had considered the steps necessary to integrate the acquisition into their organizations.

But the beat goes on. The number of failures seems to have no negative effect on the urge to merge. Deal traffic zoomed to an all-time high in 1996 (Figure 1-1), and the size of today's deals makes those of the 1980s look like small change.

Companies want growth. Their strategies call for mergers and acquisitions, and they're willing to bet on their ability to beat the odds.

MERGER/ACQUISITION MANAGEMENT CHALLENGES
Moving into New Territory

Some acquisitions are inherently much more risky than others. The more difficult ones ordinarily represent a move in new directions by the acquirer. And since they are more troublesome, the parent firm should be prepared to invest

FIGURE 1-1

M&A Activity* over the Past 10 Years

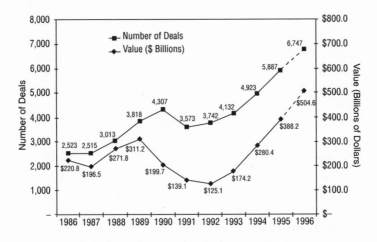

*Note: Includes all mergers, acquisitions, divestitures, and leveraged buyouts.
Source: *The Perryman Report*, September 1996, p. 1. Adapted from *Mergers & Acquisitions*.

more time, energy, and money in the integration effort. A well-crafted game plan is essential, one that is structured to deal with the predictable problems of the transition period, yet allows the flexibility necessary to accommodate contingency plans that invariably are needed.

Acquisition forays into a different industry or new line of business, for example, should be preceded by integration planning that respects the critical need to hang on to incumbents for the business savvy they possess. One management retention study has found that only one chief executive in 10 still occupied the top management job two years after his or her company was acquired.

Way back in 1981, Peter Drucker made the following comment about this risk factor in mergers / acquisitions:

"Within a year or so, the acquiring company must be able to provide top management for the company it acquired. It is an elementary fallacy to believe one can 'buy' management. The buyer has to be prepared to lose the top incumbents in companies that are bought. Top people are used to being bosses; they don't want to be 'division managers.' If they were owners or part owners, the merger has made them so wealthy they don't have to stay if they don't enjoy it. And if they are professional managers without an ownership stake, they usually find another job easily enough."

Drucker then went on to say that, "To recruit new top managers is a gamble that rarely comes off."[2] A number of years have passed since he made those observations, but his point still holds true.

Often people in *both* firms will be seriously troubled about how the acquisition may affect their personal careers. Part of the merger/acquisition planning should be aimed at deciding how these concerns will be addressed. By no means do people in the target company have a monopoly on this career uneasiness. After Novell's ill-fated merger with WordPerfect, for example, people in both organizations experienced dismay. The deal took the combined company to the brink of disaster. And after buying WordPerfect for $855 million, Novell sold it to Corel less than two years later for only $115 million—a loss of nearly three quarters of a billion dollars.

Sometimes the lack of a carefully orchestrated and closely monitored integration effort causes an impending merger to fall apart even before the final papers have been signed. A well-regarded international consulting firm of medium size reached agreement with one of the Big Six accounting firms to merge forces. Even at the outset, though, the prospect of being acquired created serious apprehension throughout the smaller organization. Things got totally out of hand when representatives of the acquirer showed up to do merger data gathering at various regional offices of the consulting firm. People at these sites got the impression they were being audited, and the resulting animosity rapidly became unmanageable. That merger was subsequently called off, but follow-up efforts by the consulting firm to merge with another suitor were complicated by the "merger hangover" resulting from the first episode. The second potential acquirer was itself a subsidiary of a much larger parent company in still another business, and personnel in the consulting firm, still gun-shy about how they had been blitzed by the "auditors," were leery of any other linkups.

Culture Shock

Corporate culture may be a rather amorphous concept, but its influence is pervasive. Organizations that appear to be highly compatible and that seemingly should be able to achieve valuable merger synergies can have underlying cultures that seriously threaten coexistence.

Corporate culture is a peculiar blend of an organization's values, traditions, beliefs, and priorities. It is a sociological dimension that shapes management style as well as operating philosophies and practices. It helps determine what sort of behavior is rewarded in an organization, whether the rewards are tangible (salary, bonuses, promotions, perquisites, and so on) or intangible (respect, access to information, power, and so on). An organization's culture helps establish the norms and unwritten rules that guide employee actions. It legitimizes certain behavior and attitudes while disaffirming others.

In merger scenarios where markedly different cultures collide, employees find that behavior once sanctioned is no longer rewarded, maybe not even approved of, and perhaps may be even punished. The measuring stick invariably changes and, of course, new people are involved in taking the measurements. Incumbents are put on the defensive as they anticipate a threat to their corporate values and organizational lifestyle. As priorities blur and inconsistencies appear between new approaches and the old way of doing business, culture shock sets in. People first become confused, then frustrated, then resistant to change.

The conventional viewpoint is that the downhill slide of Pan American World Airways, Inc., was precipitated and complicated by its acquisition of National Airlines, Inc., a company with a very different culture. Efforts to blend the workforces met with incredible resistance and bred severe morale problems. Productivity and profitability declined steadily as negative employee attitudes were reflected in weaker job performance and in customer-relations problems.

The potential for these problems is compounded when the merger involves international partners. Japan's invasion of Hollywood began in the late 1980s but was considered a financial disaster by the early 1990s. Sony Corporation and Matsushita Electric Industrial Company bought Columbia/Tristar and MCA, respectively, as a way to leverage their technology in the entertainment industry. Unfortunately the consensus-building cultures of the Japanese companies were not ready for the ego-driven, aggressive, deal-making environment of Hollywood. Rather than continue to invest more money, Sony wrote down over $3 billion of a $6 billion investment, and Matsushita sold MCA to Seagrams.

Some acquirers circumvent problems related to cultural differences by permitting their acquisitions to remain as freestanding operations with only minimal influence or involvement of the parent company. In many situations, however, that approach simply is not feasible. For example, the economies of scale that could be accomplished by merging two organizations may justify the efforts associated with reconciling cultural differences. But in those circumstances, a part of the integration strategy should be aimed at addressing cultural issues.

Sometimes one or both of the organizations involved desperately need a culture change to remain competitive. In that case, the merger event can provide an excellent window of opportunity to alter the "corporate personality." Because a merger produces so much destablization—and since it primes people to expect change—management can seize the moment and achieve significant cultural shifts.

This requires purposeful, well-executed moves, however, plus a good sense of urgency.

When the huge Tenneco, Inc., conglomerate acquired Houston Oil and Minerals Corporation, it made the time-worn pledge to keep the companies separate. But, as often found, it was a promise on which the acquirer could not deliver. Houston Oil and Minerals personnel found that being governed by one of the country's biggest conglomerates meant they had to contend with a highly structured, bureaucratic parent firm that operated through a strict chain of command. The emphasis on budgeting and forecasting created massive amounts of paperwork. Incumbents complained about the system being impersonal as well as extremely frustrating, and Tenneco's insistence on a more cautious exploration program added to people's ire. Houston Oil and Minerals had a casual, freewheeling culture that nurtured aggressiveness and rewarded entrepreneurial spirit. The dramatic differences in corporate personality and organization structure caused people to leave in droves. Tenneco reportedly made a respectable effort to hang on to Houston Oil and Minerals employees but in the end felt compelled to renege on its earlier commitment. A company memo explained that because of the loss of 34 percent of Houston Oil and Minerals management, 25 percent of its exploration staff, and 19 percent of its production people, it was impossible for the acquisition to remain a distinct unit.

Perhaps Tenneco could have done a better job of planning its postacquisition strategy. At the very least, it should have shown greater respect for the way the merger integration activities intruded on the corporate culture of the target firm. One of the most common merger problems—and one that is apparent here—is the "violation of expectations" that alienates people in the acquisition. An acquirer raises false hope by assuring incumbents that nothing will change and that they will be allowed to conduct business as usual. Then the cultural conflicts begin to surface, antagonism toward the parent company mounts, and the risk of merger failure increases.

Variations in Operating Style

Companies can experience a very difficult postacquisition adjustment process simply as a result of having different operating styles. Cultural variations may not be pronounced per se. But, for example, if one organization is highly decentralized and the other is accustomed to strong centralized control, there will be problems to work through. Operating strategies and practices of the two parties to the merger/acquisition can vary in a variety of other ways, too. Naturally, the more discrepancies that exist and the more pronounced these are, the greater the risk of failure. Integration strategies should be planned with the following thoughts in mind:

1. People, quite possibly in both companies, will be threatened and frustrated. The longer this emotionalized atmosphere lasts, the more damage it does to productivity and profitability.

2. Training will be necessary if the acquired firm's modus operandi must conform to parent company practices.

3. Employees adjust better if they are given a good rationale for making the operating changes.

4. Top management should analyze whether there really is a need to reconcile the two approaches. This requires systematic data gathering and deliberation.

5. Top management should understand that speedy integration helps people adapt to the required changes.

Employees in a company that has been led by a single dominant figure, perhaps an owner/entrepreneur, frequently feel lost when the company is acquired by a large, impersonal, and highly diversified conglomerate. Likewise, a loosely managed, highly individualistic firm has a wrenching adjustment process once it weds a bureaucratic and highly structured organization.

Westinghouse Electric Corporation, an active acquirer, submits that it has been overwhelmingly unsuccessful in its efforts to retain the entrepreneurial owner/manager of the small and medium-sized business. A company paper states:

> The reason is not difficult to see. At the same time that we provide such a man with independent, moderate to substantial wealth, we impose upon him seemingly onerous constraints on his freedom to run "his" business as he had previously done. Overcoming having given that person both the motive and the means to leave you requires strong action if it is to be successful.

Situations like these call for the integration strategy to include coaching for parent company executives on how to make entry into the acquisition. It only takes a couple of false starts (for example, confusion regarding reporting relationships and lines of authority) and the slightest display of arrogance or insensitivity for complications to develop. Westinghouse feels that its success in securing the long-term commitment of current owner/managers is directly proportionate to the amount of time it spends during *negotiations* on the following:

1. Talking to the owners about Westinghouse's expectations for the business.
2. Listening carefully to their stated expectations.
3. Discussing alternatives and contingencies.

4. Above all else, describing fully and fairly the management controls, procedures, delays, and frustrations they may encounter after Westinghouse assumes control.

MANAGEMENT HEADACHES

Management of virtually any business enterprise will find there is no shortage of problems to contend with at each stage of the organization's life cycle. Whether it be the start-up of a new venture, the struggle during the early years to establish a niche in the marketplace, the effort of a mature firm to fend off aggressive new competition, or the trials of managing mergers and acquisitions, the people in charge have their work cut out for them. But in making an acquisition, not only do top executives end up buying someone else's problems, the merger event creates a host of new headaches as well.

CHAPTER 2

A Classification of Merger/Acquisition Climates

A categorization of different merger/acquisition situations makes it much easier for management to anticipate the problems that are most likely to occur. Four distinct acquisitional postures can be identified (see Figure 2-1). Each one has its idiosyncrasies plus unique implications regarding how management should gear up to cope with the difficulties that routinely develop.

The four broad categories of mergers are rescues, collaborations, contested situations, and raids. As Figure 2-1 shows, the rescue represents the most cooperative interface between acquirer and target company. At the other end of

FIGURE 2-1

Acquisition Postures

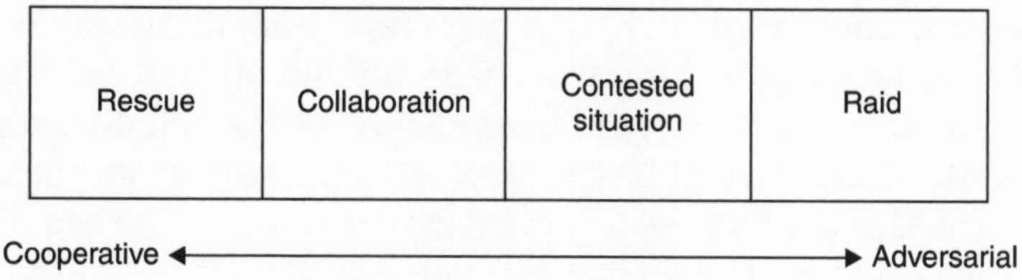

Rescue	Collaboration	Contested situation	Raid

Cooperative ◄──────────────────────────────► Adversarial

the continuum is the corporate raid, the most adversarial takeover situation. All four scenarios create adjustment problems for the acquisition. But the nature of the takeover determines to a large extent how severe the blow is, how long the trauma lasts, and the extent of damage to corporate health.

THE RESCUE

Actually, there are two different types of rescue operations. Frequently, a rescue develops in response to a raid that has been initiated by another firm, sending the target company executives scurrying in search of a "white knight." The second type of rescue occurs as a financial salvage operation. In both situations, the to-be-acquired firm is casting about for help, looking for relief of some sort. The purchasing firm, therefore, is basically viewed as a welcome party. Still, there are almost always some mixed feelings on the part of the firm being acquired. Being rescued ordinarily is just the lesser of two evils, not what the target company would choose if it had any good alternatives.

Looking for Daddy Warbucks

The organization problems and management actions in the white knight scenario are very different from the Daddy Warbucks situation. Here the acquired firm is on the brink of financial disaster, or at least suffering from a lack of key resources (usually monetary). The very nature of the problem suggests that the company has some significant weaknesses. There probably have been fundamental mistakes in the way the organization has been run. Incumbent management usually has to stand responsible for the negative state of affairs and cannot be counted on to turn things around.

Odds are that the top management team in the acquisition has already taken its best shot at running the company.

Otherwise, the firm would not have gone looking for a financial savior in Daddy Warbucks. The obvious question then becomes, "If these managers are responsible for bringing their company to this dire point and have proved incapable of overcoming problems of their own making, should they be entrusted with the husbandry of any new funds Daddy Warbucks invests in it?" The acquiring organization may be quite flush, but who wants to throw good money after bad?

In this rescue operation, quite a few members of the existing management team may be politely asked to leave. Naturally, there is fear in the hearts of some executives when it becomes obvious that an unknown number of people occupying the management ranks will likely be replaced. Employees in the acquired firm sense an acute loss of leadership, too, as their familiar standard-bearers leave the scene. Employees are understandably threatened by the prospect that the new owner may choose to deal with the financial problems by such actions as selling off a division, shutting down a plant, doing away with two layers of management, or cutting back the overall workforce by a large percentage. These are logical concerns.

This type of rescue is one of the two merger situations that require the most intervention by the parent firm. On one hand, people in the acquired company realize that things have reached the point where sacrifices will have to be made to be merged by rescue. And the people in charge have decided that the trade-offs tilt in favor of being taken over by another organization. But there are always some employees who feel they would have been better served by not being acquired. They would prefer to stake their chances on surviving through alternative means. Thus, even the most benevolent Daddy Warbucks is likely to meet with varying levels of resistance in carrying out the financial rescue.

If the acquired firm is on its last financial leg, the rescue may generate a broadly felt sense of relief. Morale may improve. A new sense of challenge and anticipation may be

apparent and certainly should be capitalized on by the acquirer. But at the same time, the parent company should (1)
gear up to cope with pockets of resistance and (2) be prepared
to counteract feelings of excessive dependency on the part of
other personnel.

When a financially ailing company goes looking for
Daddy Warbucks, the acquirer certainly needs to know the
extent of its own resources. It needs to respect the limits of
its ability to invest money and management in the new
acquisition. Invariably, some type of rehabilitation, often a
substantial degree of organizational change, is required. So,
although the rescued firm may come at a bargain price, it
usually carries hefty risks as well.

In this rescue exercise, the two companies do cooperate
to a high degree and enter into the merger by mutual prefer-
ence. But the target company is still, in a sense, a vanquished
firm. There are likely to be tender egos resulting from this,
together with a prevailing sense of defeat throughout the
organization. In this atmosphere, there is a critical need for
Daddy Warbucks to do more than tighten things up financially or even throw some new money around. People in the
acquired organization need help in rebuilding their corporate self-esteem. Their pride needs to be restored and their
motivation regenerated. They need strong leadership and a
well-defined sense of direction. And with all of this, the
sooner the better.

Rescue by the White Knight

In this scenario, we find the target company running for
cover. It's a panic situation; and under careful scrutiny, the
outcome usually carries the telltale signs of decisions based
on expediency. Time pressures rarely permit adequate
analysis of the situation. The people in charge do a poor job
of weighing the pros and cons and fall short in terms of
searching for alternatives.

To get a quick gauge of the sort of problems this situation produces, think of it as involving impulse buying and panic selling. To begin with, this suggests that many important issues get glossed over in both parties' haste to justify and finalize the deal. And since there is such a shortage of data gathering and critical thought beforehand, there has to be much more of it after the purchase has been consummated. When the smoke clears, permitting a more relaxed and objective appraisal of all aspects of the situation, the flaws in the fabric of the agreement become much more visible. Now it's time for the selling firm to begin second-guessing the wisdom of moving so rashly in the direction of the new parent company. Meanwhile, the white knight may begin to suffer buyer's remorse.

One of the large mergers of the 1980s involved Conoco, Inc., Seagram, Mobil Oil Corporation, and E. I. Dupont deNemours & Company. With two corporate raiders and a white knight involved, it appeared there was something for everyone. Certainly the stakes were high, but it was not a case where the winner took all. Conoco scrambled to elude the corporate clutches of first Seagram and then Mobil Oil, but the aftermath provided hard data that rescue has its own risks. DuPont prevailed in its offer, only to find its own independence threatened by possible loss of control to Seagram. Top management had to face a barrage of criticism from shareholders who were irate about their sagging stock prices. DuPont looked uneasily at its bankers and delicately pleaded for peace with Seagram, still a major stockholder. Meanwhile Conoco employees began to reassess their careers and wonder who would be the first to go, as it was apparent that the new owner would be divesting certain parts of Conoco in an effort to improve the financial picture.

Certainly this type of rescue is likely to generate many postmerger surprises. Quite a few significant issues that are not addressed or that are inadequately dealt with during the negotiations remain to be hammered out by the two firms.

Usually both the rescuer and the acquired firm find themselves having to make compromises nobody foresaw. Ground rules that were not established regarding how the two firms will live together have to be determined. And whereas before the papers were signed everyone seemed quite cooperative and eager to strike an agreement, now the gears seem to grind much more slowly, and a far more cautious spirit prevails.

Often the management teams from both organizations feel compelled to strengthen their respective firm's position, realizing they may have acted a bit rashly in their haste to make the deal acceptable to each other. The acquired firm, in particular, is prone to feel in retrospect that the new sense of safety came at too dear a cost. Personnel in the rescued company show an almost immediate transition from a sense of relief to wariness. Throughout the organization, people begin to wonder, "What have we done?" Now that the fearsome threat of the corporate raider has been eliminated, increasing prominence is given to the new threat that the white knight will take advantage of the situation.

So the white knight rescue is a little too much like a weekend Reno marriage. Without the traditional courtship period where people (or companies) have more opportunity to get to know each other and work through important differences, the "little period of adjustment" that routinely goes with marriage can become a long, drawn-out, and gut-wrenching experience. It is worth remembering that quick marriages are typically the hardest to make work.

In the aftermath of the white knight rescue, there is a powerful need for top management to take steps that ensure the two organizations will get to know each other. There will be a need to work through the many aspects of how the two companies will interact. This may point to the value of analyzing the compatibility of the two firms' different cultures, operating practices, and the like.

Undoubtedly, top management needs to work hard to sell the idea of the acquisition to people in both companies. Finally, the white knight rescue needs to be viewed as one of the rare acquisitions where the parent company might—just might—take a hands-off stance for an indefinite period of time. Certainly if the new acquisition is a successful, smoothly running operation, extreme care should be exercised in the way it is handled.

COLLABORATION

By far, the biggest percentage of acquisitions fall into the category of collaboration. One company wants to buy and the other company wants to sell or is persuaded to sell, so both parties approach the bargaining table of their own choosing. It is not a situation like the rescue or raid, where one of the firms has its back to the wall and ends up with a new parent.

Other identifying characteristics of the collaboration are that the acquirer does not use surprise tactics on the target firm, nor are heavy-handed measures used. Rather, both parties strive to employ diplomacy, goodwill, and negotiating finesse in striking a deal that represents a fair exchange. Usually, the negotiations are carried out with mutual respect and strong interest in doing business with each other.

These are important points because with more goodwill going into the efforts in the negotiating stages, there is likely to be more of a positive atmosphere as the two companies come out of the deal.

Johnson & Johnson is one acquisition-minded company that has consistently applied a collaborative approach. Management has chosen to go after friendly deals. One of the major dividends of this strategy is that Johnson & Johnson has developed a reputation as a very desirable suitor. Companies approach Johnson & Johnson, asking to be acquired by an outfit that's built a name for itself because it treats people well and lets them run their own deals to an unusual degree.

Johnson & Johnson seems to have judiciously weighed the pros and cons of the various acquisition tactics and decided to follow the straight and narrow path of collaboration. This sort of merger/acquisition scenario provides a pretty respectable base from which to build. There will always be some ambivalence or mixed feelings on the part of the firm being acquired, but overall the positives are viewed as outweighing the negatives. Collaboration is a pretty nonadversarial situation.

Why is it, then, that employee concerns are still so much of a problem? For one thing, the people at the top may be sold on the deal, but no one takes the trouble to sell it to the people below. It may represent a win-win proposition for the two companies, but top management should never assume this is understood by people who have not been privy to the negotiating sessions wherein the agreement was engineered.

It is almost impossible to overcommunicate in the merger arena. Obviously, top management must employ discretion and a careful sense of timing in the handling of certain information, and it is risky to make very many promises or strong statements. But apart from that, usually the more information that can be shared, the better. It is difficult to find a company in the stages of being acquired that could not benefit from a better communication process.

Collaborative mergers and acquisitions are often jarring experiences because of poor follow-up management. In other words, while there was good negotiation, there is bad integration. The delicate footwork manifested in the sensitive process of making the deal disappears. Parent company management may breathe a sigh of relief with the opportunity to get back to "business as usual." But people in the acquired firm know it's a new ball game. They are like a raw nerve with regard to how they are being handled by the new owner, who so characteristically quits tiptoeing too soon.

Collaboration ordinarily involves the most courtship. In fact, the pacing is part of the collaboration itself. As a well-known executive in one of the country's most acquisition-minded conglomerates said, "Timing is everything." If the acquirer pushes too hard, a raid can develop. The timing has to please both parties, and as a rule, intensive efforts go into talking through the marriage plus the plans for the post-merger relationship. Generally speaking, collaboration—more than any of the other categories—is a merger condition in which the autonomy of the acquired company is most likely to be preserved.

Usually there is less need for intervention on the part of the parent. Thus, in this merger situation, the conditions are most appropriate for "management deals"—contractual arrangements designed to retain key executives.

Because of these practices, the mergers that come about through collaboration typically suffer the least from "post-merger drift," the customary sag in productivity, morale, and operating effectiveness. Both parties to the merger have more ownership of the decision and therefore more commitment to making it all work.

This also suggests, however, that the acquired firm could be quite resistant to changes or interventions designed unilaterally by the new owner. Such intervention is usually perceived as an oppressive, inequitable move that violates the collaborative spirit that first gave rise to the merger. It is somewhat ironic in that the collaborative precedent established early on hints that this is the way the two firms are going to relate as time goes by. But it is unlikely that the parent company management will want (or be able) to interact with the acquisition in a collaborative manner under all circumstances. So when the precedent is not followed, management in the new acquisition gets jumpy as well as defensive. Since lower-level people in the acquisition are carefully watching their superiors, they too begin to resonate with the same negative vibrations. This sort of "collaboration backlash" is a phenomenon that acquirers will find almost impossible to avoid entirely.

THE CONTESTED SITUATION

The distinguishing difference between this acquisition approach and collaboration is that here only one of the two parties has a strong interest in making the deal, or the two firms want very different deals. Also, a contested situation may develop when there are multiple suitors who keep upping the ante for a target company. Often the firm under consideration is a reluctant bride but is unable to successfully defend itself against a takeover. The 1996 battle over Conrail provides a typical example. CSX seemed to be on the inside track, with merger negotiations proceeding peacefully. Then Norfolk Southern derailed the deal with a competing $10.4 billion bid that won shareholder approval. Conrail and CSX were left wondering who would end up owning what.

In contested situations, the negotiating can become very aggressive. There is plenty of resistance, but it is more depersonalized than that found in the raid. Here, the battling between the two firms remains more logic-based and not as emotional as it is in the raid.

Probably the major difference between these two most adversarial takeovers, though, is that in the contested situation there is less of a feeling that there is a victor and a vanquished. It is common for both parties to walk away basically content with the deal they strike. In that regard, it remains primarily a win-win encounter, and the aftermath reflects an important spirit of cooperation. There well may be a strong flavor of opportunism in the behavior of both sides to the merger equation. But in contrast to the raid, the contested situation gives management in the target company a much better chance to emerge as heroes rather than as martyrs or losers.

By the time the deal has been finalized, however, the troops in the acquired firm often are quite battle weary. The bidding contest that marks this merger fray can be very stressful and unsettling. Ambiguity mounts quickly, and employees have a tendency to lose their job concentration as they watch all the fireworks. Concern for their own careers can become quite intense if a company vying for control implies that a takeover would be followed by divestitures, shutdowns, consolidations, or layoffs. The contested situation, like the three other merger types, typically produces a slowdown in productivity and organizational momentum even *before* a deal is consummated. Almost all merger / acquisition environments give "people problems" a head start on management.

The bidding process for the *Chicago Sun-Times* created precisely this kind of turmoil. A local investor group headed by James Hogue (the incumbent publisher) saw its offer being shunned in favor of a higher bid by Australian publisher Rupert Murdoch. A few months earlier, the owners had stated that Murdoch would be an unacceptable bidder, but apparently his higher offer proved a persuasive argument. Still a third would-be buyer emerged at the last minute with an even higher bid, but that overture got a cool reception. As the acquisition contest wore on, employees first became distracted, then worried about major staff cutbacks that were rumored, and finally openly critical of the impending sale to Murdoch. Pessimism led to a wait-and-see attitude and fomented a rapidly building atmosphere of resistance throughout the workforce.

Contested acquisitions, together with some rescues and most raids, generate enough stir to get quite a bit of attention. Frequently, a few of the heads that are turned belong to executive recruiters. And in all the commotion of a contested situation or a raid, in particular, the search consultant often finds several high-talent executives with a rapidly growing interest in considering career opportunities elsewhere. This can help create a talent drain and leadership vacuum that cripple the acquired firm's effectiveness in the postmerger environment.

THE RAID

Probably no one would choose the hostile takeover route as a preferred method for making an acquisition. Now and then, an executive may be invigorated by the thrill of the chase, and it can feel good to come out on top. But the headaches usually outweigh the ego gratifications.

In this merger scenario, the adversarial climate is at its peak, with the result being maximum resistance on the part of the target firm. Typically, an intense emotional component is interjected into the battle for ownership. Often, the defense becomes desperate. The propaganda mills in both companies pump out charges and countercharges. It is bad enough that accurate communication is a scarce commodity even in the most benevolent acquisition environment. Here, the truth gets stretched ridiculously out of shape, and the rumor mill roars out of control.

A routine practice is for management in the besieged organization to generate strong antagonism among its employees toward the corporate raider. Invariably, the employees seem to love it. They defiantly wave their own corporate flag, rallying behind their leaders and becoming even more cohesive in the struggle against a common, outside enemy. This interesting phenomenon occurred in response to Wells Fargo's takeover attempt involving First Interstate Bank in California. Target company management proclaimed that the merger would have a disruptive effect on employees, hurt morale, and create an uncertain future for the firm. Then First Interstate went even further, soliciting reinforcements from politicians, employees, customers, and the media.

Employees protested on the steps of city hall and petitioned the mayor's office in Los Angeles, attempting to keep Wells Fargo from completing its bid. The merger fight was a draining, expensive, bitterly fought duel. And though Wells Fargo won the battle, the war obviously was not over. Next came the subtle resistance, the guerrilla warfare in the corporate underground.

It is true, however, that when this sort of defense works, it can be a very positive event for the target company. A more intense corporate spirit develops, and management emerges with stronger backing from the employees than it had before the raid commenced. Workers swell with enhanced pride, and morale ordinarily notches up.

The target company's executives can almost always whip up strong employee concern and bitter resistance to the takeover. The risk inherent in this defense tactic is substantial, though, as the warnings top management gives to its workforce can be a self-fulfilling prophecy if the hostile takeover is successfully accomplished by the raider. The scary scenarios target company executives develop in playing to their people's fears are potential attitudinal monsters; management's creation, they sometimes become management's curse.

When the fierce defense fails, many problems develop out of the residual antipathy. The hard-fought battles usually leave behind a lot of wreckage. Employees cannot make the psychological shifts necessary to go blithely from battle to brotherhood in a few days.

The raid creates winners and losers, but it does not necessarily end the fight. Long after the legal documents have been signed and media attention has faded away, the war may continue. So there is a catch-22 to the corporate raid, and it goes like this: Acquiring a company to sustain growth and nurture the corporate base, when undertaken through hostile action, creates negative management conditions that actually hamper expansion. The defense designed to ward off a corporate raider does not vanish in the event that it fails. The minefield planted to protect against the acquirer remains to plague management in both companies.

Top management in the newly acquired firm finds itself in somewhat of a box. Having led a very antagonistic, emotional battle against the company that is now the new parent organization, the management team that has been taken over must either recant, thereby losing credibility, or resign. In either event, the leadership of the acquired company is in trouble. As in war, the leader of a conquered company must try to alleviate the enmity and adversarial climate that he or she has orchestrated. The other alternative is to abdicate leadership.

In corporate wars, the best and brightest often flee to friendlier settings. Talent leaves first in the aftermath of hostile acquisitions, and these organizational refugees may leave behind only a shell of a management team and a workforce plagued by resentment and uncertainty. Even in amiable acquisitions, "people problems" rank right up at the top along with negative economic conditions as a prime reason for merger tangles. Resisted takeovers are even more prone to human-resource failure.

Top management in the parent company also finds itself in some operational straitjackets. On one hand, there is a need for fence mending. But because the newly acquired managers and employees are somewhat recalcitrant and begrudging, they require more policing. So the raider is often compelled to impose tighter controls and send in its own managers to function as "occupation troops." That can further alienate and demoralize target company personnel, however, resulting in management bailouts and sabotaged productivity. Corporate raiders might wish to bolster morale by promising their new corporate roommates that "management will not be changed, things will remain the same, it will be business as usual." It would be nice if things could operate like that because in hostile takeovers employees are especially sensitive to restructuring.

But it is the very thing employees make more necessary by their unwillingness to adapt.

The raiding company implicitly sets a management philosophy through the way in which it captures its quarry. In essence, the raider has made a "corporate intervention" even before it actually succeeds in the takeover. A management policy has already been demonstrated by the acquirer. Thus, it becomes very difficult to collaborate after the raid has been carried out. Management in the parent company is making a very hollow statement when it assures everyone "We don't plan to make any changes." In reality, the changes have already begun. The target company has to make quick changes in some of its behavior because of the acquisition threat. And the premerger climate virtually guarantees that further changes will be forthcoming in the postmerger period.

THE INCLINE OF RESISTANCE

The degree of resistance to the acquisition becomes greater as one moves from a relatively cooperative merger to the more adversarial events. The incline of resistance demonstrates (1) the intensity of opposition to the other party's merger objectives and (2) the amount of resources (money, energy, time, and so on) expended struggling with the merger event (see Figure 2-2).

Both the acquirer and the acquiree demonstrate forces of resistance that range from negligible to extreme. A company being rescued, as a whole, usually welcomes the acquirer. Even within the rescue, however, there will be at least passive resistance to doing things a new way. Furthermore, some people in the target firm will invariably oppose the idea of running into the arms of Daddy Warbucks or a white knight.

The incline of resistance peaks out in the hostile, defensive environment of a raid, and parent company management needs to be able and ready to meet this challenge.

FIGURE 2-2

The Incline of Resistance

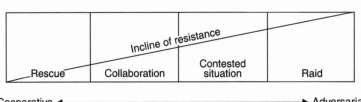

Obviously, much more will be required of parent company management in acquisitions where the incline of resistance is most pronounced. A collaborative acquisition might prove to be a successful venture, whereas a hostile takeover of the same firm might lead to failure.

As the incline mounts, both initial negotiation strategies and eventual integration policies must change. The more resistance increases, the more people on each side become one-sided. That is, they become more attached to and have more personally invested in their particular side of the issues. This is just one of the common sociological aspects of mergers and acquisitions.

The higher the incline of resistance goes because of the nature of the acquisition environment, the longer it usually takes for that resistance to subside. Raids and contested situations usually involve the most prolonged postmerger period of opposition. Those two types of takeovers call for the most concerted efforts by parent company management to alleviate the problems. Ordinarily a one-shot attempt will not be sufficient to overcome the polarization and adversarial hangover that remain. Instead, management should design a strategic integration program that respects the magnitude of the problems and that holds promise for getting people from both firms to the point of pulling together for the good of the merged firms.

THE RISK CURVE

While the incline of resistance steadily increases from the rescue type of acquisition through the raid situation, the amount of financial risk that management has to contend with tends to be greater at each end of the acquisitional continuum. In the rescue, the acquirer gains a firm that is often beset by financial woes and possesses a dearth of leadership.

The raid situation almost guarantees overt resistance and threats of bailouts by the most capable people within the organization. At a time when top talent is needed to stabilize a company acquired through hostile action, those people look elsewhere for career opportunities.

In the rescue event, it is less likely that people will leave. Unfortunately, incompetent individuals who have created the conditions necessitating a rescue are sometimes difficult to dismiss. Rather than demonstrating explicit hostility toward the acquirer, companies being rescued often have a workforce characterized by passivity and inertia. And just as that contingent of people demonstrated a prior inability to turn things around on their own, they frequently prove to have real difficulty adapting to the needed changes once new management takes over.

The risk curve (see Figure 2-3) may be misleading on one point—all acquisitions involve financial risk. Collaborative or contested acquisitions can result in financial failures, just as can rescues or raids. This curve assumes that, all things being equal with regard to the external economic climate, the risks of failure are greater with the rescue or raid situation than they are with either of the other two merger classifications.

Corporate raiders often have to spend more than would be desired to obtain a reluctant firm and thus become financially threatened by the debt burden that must be assumed. Also, the resistance gradient is at its highest point in the raiding scenario, and employee resistance can sabotage even

FIGURE 2-3

The Risk Curve

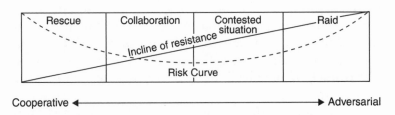

Cooperative ◀————————————————————▶ Adversarial

a fairly well-financed takeover. In the more cooperative rescue mode, risk is great because of the nature of the takeover.
It often involves saving a company that is flirting with insolvency or that must shore up sagging or departing leadership.
The vitality of such a firm is seriously in question.

NEGATIVE SYNERGY OF MERGERS

A common argument offered in favor of mergers and acquisitions is that a positive synergistic linkup can be achieved.
Company A buys Company B, and their combined resources
represent more than the sum of their individual parts. The
synergistic sword cuts both ways, however, and the down-
side risks typically are not explored in as much depth as the
upside potential.

Regrettably, two companies' problems can be just as
synergistic as their potentials. One firm's difficulties plus the
ailments of the other cannot be conveniently added up to a
neat sum total. The merger brings with it a new and unique
set of previously nonexistent difficulties.

Over the years, top-management teams have been
prone to disregard the negative synergy of mergers in their
strategic planning relative to growth by acquisition. Corporate planners focus their analysis primarily on what the
buyer and the target company can each bring to the merger,

with little formal study being aimed at ascertaining what the merger event itself will do. In fact, the merger is a corporate intervention. It should be respected as a new force that management must contend with. At times, it stands as a rather cataclysmic influence. When the decision to acquire or merge is first being made, those realities do not exist. But newly forged corporate bonds bring new realities and a fresh set of facts.

Management in the acquiring company should take pains to play out various merger scenarios in careful detail. More thought and war gaming should be devoted to an analysis of how the companies can be combined. Contingency planning should be expanded to take into fuller account the negative synergy that may develop.

This is particularly true in the corporate raid because in the hostile takeover the two parties are not working together in a collaborative fashion at all. They are not putting their heads together to figure out how to make the deal work. Thus, contingency planning is extremely one-sided. The acquiring company—and for that matter, the target company as well—must lean much too heavily on conjecture. It is bad enough if the adversary does not work *with* you. In the raid, the adversary is working *against* you. Each party to the merger throws surprises into the situation. Each company is at odds with the other's line of reasoning. Both parties are out to confound the other's strategies.

Ordinarily, merger planning and decision making are based most heavily on the financial considerations involved. But the success or failure hinges very heavily on the intentions of both sides in the equation. And in a hostile takeover attempt, neither one of the management teams has sufficient insight into the intentions of the other. This makes it extremely difficult to predict what's coming.

CHAPTER 3

Psychological Shock Waves of Mergers and Acquisitions

When merger rumblings are heard in the organizational jungle, the natives get restless. The work climate changes. This change is a given. It is not something that top management in the acquiring firm can allow or prevent at will. The magnitude of change can be controlled to some extent. But whether or not there is change at all simply is not subject to debate. Everyone who will be affected by the merger / acquisition—and top management in particular—should accept this fact and concentrate on how to come to grips with it.

Effective management of mergers and acquisitions demands that the people in charge be prepared for the emotional shake-up accompanying this kind of organizational growth. When word goes out that an acquisition is in the wind, there is a measurable impact on employee attitudes, feelings, and work behavior. The regrettable fact is that these shifts or changes—again, unavoidable—are for the most part negative. They reflect how a distressing psychological event has affected the lives of executives, managers, and the rank and file. Usually people in both companies, but particularly the one being acquired, must go through a major adjustment process. They have to adapt to a variety of new organizational realities.

But people often resist change. Changes they fear or changes that are not of their own making ordinarily elicit the most resistance. This is a key point because most people whose company has merged or been acquired had no part in that decision. Not only did they have no say in the matter, they often were taken completely by surprise.

Employees commonly get blindsided, emotionally jolted, by the news that their corporate family is being reshaped and given a new authority structure. Feeling no personal ownership of the decision someone made to merge or sell the company, employees' commitment to support the idea may be weak.

The heightened state of uncertainty that is instantly created pervades the work climate. People get jumpy. They wonder when the other shoe will fall. And because they fear additional surprise—particularly regarding their own career safety—they instinctively move to protect themselves.

The merger and the potential changes it brings are resisted deliberately as well as unconsciously. Some people are very outspoken and overt in expressing their dismay. Instead of trying to conceal their opposition, they purposefully ventilate it, perhaps in hopes of short-circuiting the deal. While some choose to openly express their shock, anger, and frustration, other employees could not hide their feelings if they tried.

The unconscious resistance, far more subtle but often more pernicious and damaging in the scheme of things, is much more widespread. It is more passive in nature. It gets manifested in the job performance of people who would honestly assert that they wish to be cooperative and support the corporate marriage. But the hard facts argue convincingly that the unconscious resistance is there, and that it is taking its toll. It shows in morale, turnover statistics, productivity, loss of competitive advantage, deterioration in revenues, disappointing profits, and so on.

Even when people in the acquired firm make a concerted effort to adjust and embrace it, the merger can turn sour. Their coping behaviors tend to be highly self-oriented and thus dysfunctional as far as the organizational good is concerned. The things they do and don't do in looking out for themselves are frequently incompatible with what the organization needs from them at that time. Much employee behavior that is well-intentioned and even self-sacrificing runs counter to what needs to happen in a merger environment. But if management has not been trained to manage the change process, why should it be expected to play it by ear and get it right the first time around? Or even the second, third, or fourth time?

KEY DYNAMICS SET IN MOTION BY THE MERGER

The merger/acquisition scenario is highly predictable in terms of the psychological dynamics generated. It helps if management knows this and knows what to expect. That is at least a first step in the direction of being much better equipped to deal with the situation effectively.

The shudder that moves through an organization when it is acquired is no peculiar or unique phenomenon. It is simply human nature in action. And since organizations are made up of people, top management can anticipate the key dynamics with great certainty.

Ambiguity

As the dust begins to settle following the announcement of an impending acquisition, a powerful new force begins to register its influence. This first dynamic is a climate of ambiguity. It reveals itself as a work atmosphere wherein there are far more questions than answers. People at all levels feel it as an information vacuum. There is a disconcerting lack of clarity regarding the corporate future and the further surprises or changes it holds. People also wonder about the role they as employees may or may not play in the upcoming scheme of things.

Even if higher management tries to alleviate this uneasiness by giving assurances about job tenure, a substantial amount of tension remains as people wonder about what new requirements might be made of them, what new reporting relationships might develop, and so on. Employees generally suspect there will be some sort of change in procedures, objectives, operating style, and the management structure.

This pervasive ambiguity stems quite naturally from two roots: (1) top management's need (or felt need) to be discreet and (2) top management's own lack of specifics regarding the ramifications of the merger.

Everyone is suffering from the unknown. And the truth is that even the president and board of directors do not have the power to satisfy everyone's curiosity and rid the work environment of ambiguity. Furthermore, in many situations, top executives usually consider it injudicious, possibly unkind, and maybe even illegal to inform people of the hard facts.

So a great deal of ambiguity, vagueness, or fuzziness builds up as the merger / acquisition situation unfolds. Some people have a psychological makeup that enables them to endure this kind of work climate reasonably well. Others find it extremely upsetting. Those employees who like order, generous job structure, a well-defined and predictable chain of command, and a clear sense of direction are inclined to feel dangerously adrift in the merger environment. All of a sudden, their world has become destabilized.

Weakening Trust Level

The second major dynamic that top management needs to understand is the lowered trust level in the company. Invariably, the announcement of merger plans will cause the affected parties to become more suspicious and wary.

One reason for this may be the rude shock often caused by the abrupt announcement of the merger. Employees quite understandably will often conclude that top management cannot be relied on to be sufficiently open and aboveboard about things that very directly affect the individual. Moreover, people at all strata in the corporate structure usually realize that the top decision makers know more than they are telling. Employees know implicitly that more surprises are forthcoming.

Personnel who previously were willing to give the company the benefit of the doubt now become skeptics, some even cynics. And those who were mistrustful or insecure to begin with may become downright antagonistic and paranoid. Those who had been quite willing to rely on top management to look out for the needs and interests of the average employee now feel obliged to change their perspective. Now everything that is done or said by key executives gets viewed with a more jaundiced eye.

Actually, this is a rational response. Weakening trust level is a monster created (and sometimes unnecessarily nurtured) by top management through faulty communication and insufficient candor. The bigger the initial shock and the greater the secretiveness, the more the trust level suffers. This leads to the third dynamic.

Self-Preservation

Merger/acquisition activity leads to self-preservation as a dominant motive in employee behavior. The weaker the trust level, the more visible the self-protective behaviors that surface. Particularly, those individuals in the middle management and executive ranks begin to deploy their personal armaments toward maximum protection of their individual careers. Rank-and-file employees may be just as troubled as those in leadership positions, but usually they give much less visible evidence of attempts to protect their jobs.

It is interesting to observe the myriad ways in which people strive to defend themselves. Some launch an aggressive attack, actively vying for position, and sometimes hoping to leverage themselves strategically into a position of even greater power and prestige. Others lie low and wait for the smoke to clear, preferring to maneuver carefully rather than attack boldly. And some calculate that their best odds for surviving will result from simply not offending. They deliberately move out of the line of fire and hope that fate smiles on them.

At any rate, self-protective behaviors result in many hidden agendas. These divert time and energy from the pursuit of company objectives. Also, top management finds it more difficult to direct an effective corporate offensive because all of a sudden it is much harder to predict what people will do. Employee behavior is founded much more on emotion and obscure motives, less on apparent logic or rational thought.

THE EMOTIONAL IMPACT ON PEOPLE

Human beings instinctively seek to maintain control and predictability over their world and their immediate environment. The more ambiguous the work climate is, as in a merger, the more this human goal is sabotaged. High levels of ambiguity lead to excessive uncertainty. Employees become confused, less sure of themselves, and sometimes highly anxious.

Even after the initial impact of the shock has diminished, employees in the acquired firm are hit with repeated demands for change and adaptation. This invariably disrupts their established and previously successful adjustment to life, as they are beset by financial concerns, professional insecurities, and fear of the new as well as the unknown. These uncertainties, fears, and inner tensions do distinct damage to individual productivity. Regrettably, anxiety tends not to be a very constructive emotion. It inhibits creativity, interferes with one's ability to concentrate, acts as a drain on physical energy, and frequently lowers the person's frustration tolerance. Logical thought processes give way to emotionally colored problem solving and decision making.

The impact of a lowered trust level within the corporation is similarly negative. This, too, can provoke an unhealthy degree of anxiety. Tension mounts, contributing to the psychological stress load employees have to carry. Individuals may become more fearful or noticeably more angry, hostile, and defensive. Employee morale and attitudes are corrupted by this highly contagious mind-set that ravages the workplace.

When self-preservation becomes a primary concern, employee behavior reflects selfishness at the expense of a needed concern for the organizational good. Those personnel who suffer a sense of betrayal by top management commonly transfer their loyalties. The owner or CEO who may have been an important father figure for the organization may come to be viewed as one who abandoned his people, the implication being that one is foolish to place trust in top management (particularly if top management consists of outsiders).

Sometimes these self-protective behaviors lead to a variety of regressive acts on the part of employees. For example, some people withdraw. Managers may hole up in their offices. Employees may find superiors more inaccessible and may themselves invest less effort in communicating. Workers often exhibit a greater degree of emotional detachment vis-à-vis the firm. Thus, their commitment weakens and, along with it, standards drop and output diminishes. But detachment does represent one way of protecting oneself from being taken advantage of, hurt, or surprised.

In some instances, an entire department or work group becomes more close-knit as far as its own members are concerned yet more isolated from the organizational effort as a whole.

The important thing for management (in both the acquiring and acquired firms) to remember is that these are all legitimate reactions. Obviously, they are counterproductive and do a disservice to the organization, and they frequently create even greater problems for the employee. But they are understandable and predictable in view of the key dynamics that underlie them.

NEGATIVE EFFECTS ON EMPLOYEE BEHAVIOR

As the psychological shock waves surge through the organization, they take their toll in operating effectiveness. Emotions—psychological factors—begin to bias behavior. Six major problem areas highlight the fact that top management is making a crucial error when it fails to deal expertly with the emotional issues in a merger or acquisition.

Communication Deteriorates

As the trust level in the organization drops, people begin to play their cards much closer to their chest. The information channels receive less input that is dependable. And the data that does circulate is more likely to be filtered, distorted, or edited out completely before it reaches its intended destinations.

It seems that virtually everyone has an increased appetite for information and a diminished willingness to feed honest, accurate data to others. Rumors rush in to fill the communication vacuum that develops. There is no overall shortage of information, but much of what is there in abundance is erroneous, mere speculation, or both.

This problem of information warp is compounded by people's exaggeration, fear mongering, and wishful thinking. Many silly notions are passed along from person to person, frequently embellished with each retelling. The traditional rules of gossip prevail—that is, truth gets distorted, unfounded ideas are reported as established facts, insignificant matters come to sound like high drama, problems are blown out of proportion, and so on. Some people intentionally twist the truth and circulate erroneous information. Their motive may be to sandbag higher management, sabotage a peer they see as a potential competitor, or protect themselves and perhaps justify their mistakes.

The rampant mistrust, wariness, and paranoia cause people to distort a lot of what they see and hear. As people become more skeptical and cynical regarding the validity of what higher management has to say, they are inclined to misinterpret and misperceive far more than they would under ordinary circumstances. Issues are emotionalized, and that contributes to data distortion. People lose objectivity as a result of their concern and ego involvement.

Top management is likely to experience frustration regardless of how honest it tries to be in communicating with employees at the various levels in the firm. To some extent, this is because people selectively perceive. Some hear only what they want to hear or what they expect to be told. Others construe beyond what top management actually says, reading between the lines and in the process reading more into a statement than was originally intended. Hints, subtle implications, or innuendos are mentally snatched up, fleshed out in much greater detail by the person's imagination, and then thrown back in the face of the executive later on as proof of his or her lack of integrity. It is very common to observe employees mentally constructing the reality they (1) wish for or (2) fear.

It is ironic that top management probably never tries harder to be truthful than it does in the merger/acquisition arena and yet still fails. There should be little doubt that top management genuinely wants to tell the truth. But frequently executives may not know what the truth is and, as a result, catch themselves (or get caught) in duplicity. It is important to remember that employees commonly are not feeling very congenial toward the owners and top executives after the announcement that an acquisition is forthcoming. Employees are expecting more trouble. And they are expecting more surprises from the people in charge. Furthermore, when the top executives talk, everyone else in the organization hangs onto their every word. In such circumstances, it is easy for the boss to make communication mistakes.

Because of the facades, faking, outright lies, and inadvertent misunderstandings, the organizational trust level is still further diminished. Weakening trust, in turn, causes more communication damage, and the downward spiral continues.

There are other reasons for communication difficulties that develop a little further along in the takeover process. First, the communication networks tend to become more complex. More people become involved in problem solving and decision making, and this blurs the issue regarding who should be informed regarding what. Also, the communication channels typically grow longer. The distances from decision centers increase. A company traditionally may have had the benefit of an owner/operator who was always available and easily accessible for information or decisions. But if the company is sold to an acquirer with home offices two thousand miles away, it is going to become more difficult and time-consuming to transact business. As information begins to travel along different paths, it also becomes easy for some people to unintentionally get left out of the loop. This can result in the loss of crucial input and also will frequently give rise to backtracking and regrouping to get things coordinated. Finally, companies involved in the merger process often discover that they communicate in somewhat different languages. That would be enough of a problem in itself, but remember that the people in the acquired firm (or both firms, perhaps, if a full merger is to be accomplished) are suffering the additional communication problems associated with the emotional trauma they are experiencing.

Perhaps the worst thing about communication problems is that they don't just remain communication problems. They create secondary symptoms that then must be addressed.

Productivity Suffers and Momentum Sags

With self-preservation becoming a more paramount concern in the minds of employees, they become less willing to make decisions or take risks. An air of tentativeness or a wait-and-see attitude prevails. Managers and upper-level executives often move into holding patterns, deliberately choosing a play-it-safe stance. Everybody seems to feel more comfortable with the idea of making sins of omission rather than commission. Employees seem more willing to do nothing than to do wrong.

Part of the productivity loss can be attributed to people's resistance to change. Upon close scrutiny, some of that resistance actually makes pretty good sense. Employees throughout the organization simply may not know what changes are required. (Here is a good example of where the communication processes may have failed.) Others choose not to exercise initiative, possibly not even to act very vigorously on definite instructions, simply because they don't know why something is being required. People hesitate to embrace new work roles or tackle new assignments due to uncertainty regarding their own ability to make the changes. Finally, the problem is still further compounded by people not having a good understanding regarding the standards by which they will be judged.

So the big question in people's minds appears to be, "Who do I need to please?" Until that has been determined and employees have ascertained to their own satisfaction what it takes to please that person or make marks in that score book, little is going to happen. People assume a more conservative stance and are most comfortable living with the status quo.

Effective management, then, means making the acquired workforce feel secure enough to remain active, decisive, and resourceful. It means providing a good sense of direction and explaining the rationale for the course that has been charted. Finally, it means letting people know who's keeping score and how it's being kept, plus demonstrating that they have the encouragement and support of parent company management.

Parochialism Increases and Team Play Deteriorates

The merger environment frequently sees intergroup cooperation and support being sacrificed for a better-defended self or a less vulnerable in-group. This, of course, is a direct outgrowth of the lowered trust level and desire for self-preservation. If the takeover is nonhostile, and particularly if there is to be very little or no consolidating or eliminating of functions, things may proceed smoothly. But it is not unusual to find one department or work group seeking to further its cause at the expense of another. The "we" spirit can evaporate in an atmosphere where people concentrate more on tooting their own horns or protecting their flanks.

Sometimes team play suffers more within than between teams. This happens when an employee decides that individual effort is a more promising avenue than team play for making it under the new regime that is to be established. Intragroup cohesiveness may be thrown to the winds, replaced by the feeling that it is every man for himself. In that atmosphere, individual cunning displaces collaborative effort.

Postmerger studies frequently find that tasks or projects requiring mutual effort and team play have bogged down in organizational politics. Competition subverts cooperative interplay, and the overall corporate offensive suffers severely because of this splintering effect.

Power Struggles Throw Work into Disarray

At its best, a merger causes existing power networks to be reexamined and, in many instances, renegotiated. At its worst, a merger situation may deteriorate into a free-for-all as positions of authority are up for grabs. Sometimes longstanding alliances are dissolved altogether. And the old, established ways of getting things accomplished in the company simply may not work any longer.

Typically, there is some jockeying for position. The natural result is that some people lose clout. And this dilemma helps explain why employees move into holding patterns. The employee witnessing a shake-up in the power structure usually has some tough questions to face. For example, whose coattails should he or she ride? Whose star is on the rise? Which programs will survive, and which ones will go out the window?

Often there is much wasted effort. One person's pet project may lose its funding in the final stages, just when the real payoff is about to be realized. Another program may be sabotaged because its sponsor loses his or her power base in the organization. Many corporate opportunities slip past, disregarded or completely unnoticed, because managers are preoccupied with the infighting and intramural power plays.

One of the most common complaints of managers and executives whose firm has been acquired relates to their loss of autonomy and control. The adjustment can be very difficult. And until the power balance has been restructured, communicated, and actually accepted by lower-echelon personnel, organizational functioning cannot help but suffer. Unclear reporting relationships and poorly defined decision-making authority are familiar symptoms in mergers that go bad. To some extent, such problems plague almost all companies that find themselves being acquired by another organization.

Commitment Is Lost

Corporate goals and objectives ordinarily become more obscure during the period immediately preceding and following the actual merger. Even departmental objectives tend to become more indefinite, particularly in those work groups that can most likely see themselves being consolidated, reshaped, or eliminated altogether. This leads to a weakened sense of direction on the part of employees, and that in turn results in diminished commitment. Employees rarely maintain a strong drive and desire to achieve when their targets are out of focus. When the game plan gets fuzzy, as it ordinarily does in the company that has just been acquired, the players simply don't play with the same degree of intensity.

For lack of a well-orchestrated, focused effort, employee energies are diffused. The overall organization begins to drift because its various parts are not operating in a sufficiently purposeful, coordinated effort. In fact, one department or work group may be duplicating the efforts of another or, worse still, working at cross-purposes.

Management needs to remember that resources tend to gravitate toward clear goals. And if there is no well-defined sense of direction, the available resource—personnel, money, material, and time—will inevitably be underutilized and spent in ways that fall well short of producing the potential returns.

There is still another important reason for the loss of commitment that occurs on the heels of an acquisition. Employees are inclined to assume that the corporation has become preoccupied with its financial best interests rather than their individual or collective well-being. So they are inclined to grow more blasé, with their dedication and loyalty deteriorating as the natural consequence. Frequently, their leader has left the scene, too, so that the personal ties that engendered loyalty and commitment have been severed.

In many mergers, a true adversarial relationship begins to fester. People may come to perceive the situation as "me against the company." Employees routinely look at a merger as an essentially financial proposition rather than something that is done out of corporate humanitarianism. And their reaction, understandably, is to shift from a company commitment to more of a self-commitment. In the process, of course, motivation erodes further.

Employees Bail Out

The sixth major people problem created by the psychological shock waves is the "bailing out" phenomenon. The degree to which this occurs will depend heavily on the nature of the acquisition—for example, whether it was a mutually sought deal or fiercely resisted. Usually, the more antagonistic the premerger battle, the more (and the quicker) people hotfoot it out of the acquisition toward other career opportunities.

Some people scramble just to get out before the axe falls. They may view the merger as their certain demise because it means the loss of a mentor and their own "favored person" status. Some bail out because they recognize a talented counterpart in the other firm and conclude that they personally will be the one let go because of duplicated functions.

Sometimes, however, employees leave simply to escape the increasing ambiguity and intense anxiety the merger generates for them personally. Once again, some people find having to contend with a heightened state of ambiguity in their work unbearable. For these people, there is truth in the saying "The certainty of misery is better than the misery of uncertainty." In other words, better to bail out into the fire immediately than sizzle in the frying pan indefinitely. This may not make sense to the objective observer, but if emotional logic exists, perhaps it is the rationale for this sort of behavior.

Often people leave even though they personally feel very secure regarding the opportunity to keep their jobs. Their motivation can be that they envision a bleak future as they see the new corporate direction beginning to materialize. A manager in the acquired firm may lament that the company has been taken over by an outfit sure to redirect the organization away from his or her fundamental career interests. Another executive or manager may fear that the organization will be milked as a cash cow by the new parent company, thus drained of its resources and humbled before the eyes of the business world. Another person may worry about having a career stymied by a variety of new people in superior positions or peer slots, people who will be favored when promotion opportunities arise.

Some, of course, leave because they dislike the specter of encroaching controls. Faced with the possibility that they may suffer a loss of authority and decision-making latitude, they take the initiative, call it quits, and head in search of greener pastures. Sometimes it is not because they fear a loss of authority but rather because they anticipate having to adapt to different (and unpalatable) operating philosophies after the merger.

Probably the most damaging bailouts are of those executives, managers, or technical experts who resign because they do not like the prospect of being "layered down" in the organization. They foresee a loss of status together with a new set of management constraints from above. The hard fact is that frequently the good people are the ones who jump ship—those critical few who made the company a viable target for acquisition in the first place. These are the people who are the key to its present and future success. Left behind may be little but deadwood, drones, and the disheartened.

Perhaps it should be noted here, too, that bailing out is very contagious. This is primarily because the top talent—key power figures, opinion leaders, and the like—serve as important role models for the rest of the organization. When they jump ship, it legitimizes such action. More than that, it popularizes the action. Also, bailouts scare the people who are left behind and make them question the wisdom of remaining themselves. And each bailout represents just one more adjustment for the people who stay, one more point of ambiguity, one more reason to resent the new parent company.

So there are many good reasons for trying to identify accurately, and early on, just (1) who it's important to keep, (2) who is likely to leave, and (3) how those important figures can best be induced to stay with the acquisition rather than having them modeling leaving behavior that could be extremely costly.

PART TWO

Resolving Redundancies and Staffing Issues

CHAPTER 4

Three Major Sources of Management Turnover

Rule one of *Barron's* 10 Rules for Investors says, "The success of a company is dependent nine parts on management and one part on all other factors, including luck."

If that's true for companies in general, it is particularly true for firms that are being merged or acquired. As far back as the conglomerate period of the go-go 1960s, Leighton and Tod affirmed this belief in a *Harvard Business Review* article. They wrote:

> We cannot overestimate the importance of getting to know the president and his key personnel. Evidence indicates that the more fully the parent company understands their emotional and personal needs, their weaknesses and strengths, their fears and apprehensions, the more effectively it will be able to help with the acquisition and to manage the company later on.[1]

A number of pressing questions desperately need to be answered:

1. Who should stay?
2. Who should go?
3. Who shall decide, and how?

4. What new managerial demands will a merger bring about?

5. What sort of managerial efficiencies or economies of scale can be achieved?

6. What new management talents will the merger call for: market-realizing savvy, technical expertise, financial acumen, turnaround artistry, team building, a more broad-gauged perspective, fast-growth capability, management of change?

7. What kind of management potential has been acquired? And what does it imply for long-range personnel planning?

8. How can the newly acquired retinue of managers best be managed and motivated?

9. How does one play to their strengths and shore up their weaknesses?

10. Will the right personal chemistry and compatibility be there? Can I work with these people?

The answers to some of these questions, of course, hinge on other issues that must be addressed, such as the following:

1. To what extent will the organizations be merged?

2. Will the acquisition be run on a centralized basis or be allowed extensive operating autonomy?

3. What control policies and procedures will be implemented to guide the subsidiary?

4. Where operations or functions are overlapping, how will the parent company ascertain which facilities, departments, and so on, will be abolished, expanded, or left as they are?

Management should establish well-defined criteria by which to evaluate the human resource aspects of the merger. Parent company objectives must be identified as a preliminary step and conclusions drawn regarding how these objectives can best be achieved.

Assuming that the acquiring firm has developed a strategic road map that addresses the integration issues mentioned above, the next order of business is to make a thorough assessment of key management and technical talent that initially comes with a new acquisition. Part of this appraisal should be a determination of how much of this talent could be retained.

BAILOUTS

One of the most likely bailout points is in the top management ranks. Key executives who fought the merger/acquisition often feel that their relationship with the parent company has been strained beyond repair and that they have too many fences to mend. Feeling that their career is on shaky ground, and without any quick and convincing messages to the contrary from top management in the parent company, they bolt.

The acquirer is frequently taken aback by this turn of events. Parent company executives may believe the relationship is developing quite well and think they have made it plain that they bear no residual ill will. In fact, parent company management sometimes assumes it has done more than is necessary to prevent key managers in the target firm from jumping ship. But assumptions can be extremely costly when dealing with acquisitions, particularly when they lead to vacancies in some of the most critical positions.

Another source of bailouts would be the disgruntled leaders who see themselves being layered away from the top of the power structure so that they suffer a loss of authority or stature. They leave of their own volition because they dislike new reporting relationships that place them further from the top person. Sometimes, though, they jump to conclusions and part company on the basis of false rumors or their own misperceptions. In other instances, the acquirer simply fails to do an adequate selling job vis-à-vis how the new organization structure will still offer substantial challenge and, perhaps in the long run, even more career potential.

It should be obvious that these bailout candidates need their egos stroked. They need more attention, encouragement, and assurance of their value to the company than they are getting in many instances. The irony is that if they do leave and have to be replaced, the acquirer will end up having to spend much more time and likely quite a bit more money replacing them and bringing the new hires up to speed. Moreover, even when that has been accomplished, the company often has not fully replaced what the departing executives took in terms of technical knowledge, company insights, rapport with the workforce or customers, and so on.

Some people turn in their keys and credit cards in the wake of a merger even though their job is secure and they are held in high favor by the parent organization. These departures occur as the incumbents see storm clouds on the horizon regarding new operating styles or management philosophies likely to be imposed by the acquirer.

Here again, some of these people leave on impulse. Taking a fatalistic view of how they will be handled by the new owner, they clear out their desks and leave. Ordinarily, they rationalize their behavior as something that grows out of philosophical differences regarding how they feel business should be conducted. But underneath this veneer may be more fundamental psychological forces—specifically, a fear of not measuring up, concern about having an inability to meet the new standards, a reluctance to admit that they actually don't know how to do things the parent company way.

So again, ego-related issues begin to create merger problems. But the parent company is not likely to hear a key person from the acquired firm say, "Listen, I'm scared. I'm afraid I'm going to look foolish or outclassed." Pride gets in the way, and instead of a cry for help, one hears complaints and criticism aimed at the new owner. So often, people pick their words not to reveal who they really are and what they truly think but to conceal their fears and protect themselves. Parent company management often fails to perceive the dynamics at work. The needed support, encouragement, and coaching are never provided, and the person suffering the insecurities finds an escape route.

Granted, some executives who leave because they do not like the acquirer's operating style or philosophy are extremely confident, secure individuals. They harbor zero concerns about their own ability to measure up. They simply can't accept how the company is supposed to be run in the postmerger setup. Parent company efforts to keep these people on board should include a concerted communication effort. Pains should be taken to explain the new approach or methodologies—for example, the justification, the benefits, the specifics regarding how the system will work, and the important role these managers will play in the scheme of things. Naturally, some will still leave. But some will stay and adapt well, and both they and the company will benefit.

Some key players jump ship because they cannot (or will not) endure the uncertainty, ambiguity, and stress so characteristic in a new acquisition. Other people leave because they can't stand merger politics. The best way to hang on to this contingent of employees is to overcome the psychological shock waves as quickly as possible and then get people oriented toward clear, definitive goals. These people want closure. They want to know where they stand, what's expected of them, and who they will be dealing with in the months to come. The sooner this can be laid out for them, the more likely they are to decide to remain with the firm, settle down, and resume their prior level of productivity.

Executives who have been given "golden parachutes" make unusually good bailout material. Likewise, the nouveaux

riches who sold their stock and can walk away with a bundle
of money have a new found freedom. Both sets of people frequently leave the scene simply because they have a variety of
reasons for doing so, with only a few weak reasons for staying. Often the parent company bends over backward to keep
these people, only to end up with a top management team
that isn't hungry anymore. As the team's drive and motivation slacken, so do the sense of urgency and the competitive
spirit in the rest of the organization.

Finally, there are always people in an acquired firm who
seek other job alternatives because they don't like the new
corporate direction that, at least in their opinion, the merger
portends. For example, if an employee had plans of building
his or her career with a small but growing retail firm and it
is taken over by some large, stuffy, bureaucratic organization
in a completely different industry, the individual may become a bailout because of the gloomy career future she or he
foresees.

It is imperative that the parent company remember,
though, that the best people will probably find it easiest to
leave. Those who possess the most talent will, in all prob-
ability, have the greatest number of alternatives, the most
promising opportunities, dangled before them. These people
also will have the most hustle, the most personal initiative,
so they won't wait for opportunity to come knocking. And
they are not afraid to seize opportunity it even if it means
leaving familiar routines and comfortable surroundings.
Certainly, they are not averse to leaving the destabilized
atmosphere created by a merger.

TERMINATIONS

Insurgents and Obstructionists

In many merger situations, particularly the more adversarial takeovers, significant people in the acquired firm re-
fuse to embrace the new order. They are either unwilling

or unable to adapt to the new scheme of things. These people pose a problem on two counts. First, at a time when the organization needs facilitative influences, they are an obstruction. They get in the way of the needed changes, whether as a result of personal rigidity, lack of competence, or simply rebellion against the new owner. Second, they tend to become somewhat insurgent, infecting others with their negativism and resistance to change. Typically, they rationalize away their own inadequacies and project blame onto the parent company, accusing it of being responsible for the shortcomings in their job performance. They fan the flames of unrest, sometimes subtly and surreptitiously, sometimes blatantly. Particularly when in positions of authority or high visibility, they easily provoke greater discontent among other personnel. Sometimes, of course, this undesirable behavior can be eliminated if the parent company (1) gets an accurate fix on who these people are and (2) confronts the problem head-on. But while some individuals have the ability and the willingness to change their attitudes and upgrade their work behavior, others do not.

Those people who do not succeed in getting on board should be separated from the organization. When they are indulged, allowed second or third chances, or merely given a light slap on the wrist, the parent company is essentially reinforcing the wrong behavior. Much better for the acquirer to set definite limits, communicate those boundaries in a clear and distinct fashion, and then enforce them firmly. This can send an important, unmistakable message to bystanders in the acquired firm who are watching attentively to see how the new management deals with personnel problems. Not only is it important for the success of the merger that the insurgents be terminated, it is also essential that the early precedents be designed to communicate clearly the new rules or standards by which top management plans to operate.

Executives in the acquiring firm lose credibility and respect when they drag their feet in making needed terminations. Management can be firm without being ruthless, equitable without being indulgent. Such an approach is in the long-run best interest of both the organization and the employee.

Staffing Duplications

The merging of two organizations routinely creates superfluous or excess personnel as a result of the consolidation of departments, integration of functions, or elimination of certain work groups. When two companies with duplicate functions merge, obviously there are redundancies that cannot be justified from a payroll standpoint. Further, mergers are frequently sought for the economies of scale they permit, and this means that in all likelihood some people will need to be dismissed.

Ordinarily when such reorganizations are contemplated, the parent company should move expeditiously to make the realignments and complete the merger process. To begin with, people can usually sense when such a consolidation is likely, and organizational momentum suffers badly until that process has been finalized. The more quickly top management moves in, making its restructuring and staffing decisions, the more it gets to exercise its preferred options. In the early stages, the best performers are still in the picture and therefore can more likely be given key assignments sufficiently challenging to keep them with the company. On the other hand, if the reorganization and reassignments come too slowly, the acquisition frequently stalls out, and good people go elsewhere to seek their fortunes.

Nonperformers

When the acquisition of a firm is carried out as a financial salvage operation, there typically is strong logic in favor of replacing some key people. The executives who carried the organization into red ink and who are seen as part of the problem instead of the solution are obvious candidates for termination. To leave these executives at the helm may run the risk of sabotaging any turnaround effort the acquirer attempts. The tough question, and one that deserves a well-researched answer, is "Which incumbents should be retained for the contribution they could make to the ailing firm's rehabilitation?"

Even those acquired firms that are financially sturdy will often have selected personnel who, for one reason or another, are not performing up to par. Perhaps they were indulged by the company for one reason or another, managed to escape notice somehow, or led a charmed life that allowed them to survive without really earning their keep. Under the more scrutinizing, nonpartisan eye of management in the new parent company, however, these people will be found wanting and should be encouraged to leave.

There are several good reasons for moving promptly to separate these employees. First, if they are not contributing that much, better to let them go and remove that drain on the payroll. Second, this action communicates a worthwhile message to others throughout the acquisition to the effect that the new owner has little tolerance for nonperformance. This sort of termination gets the word across that mediocrity can be a risk to job security. A third argument supporting the idea of expeditiously terminating weak people is that such action generally is applauded by those in the acquired firm who are good performers. The capable people, those who are really productive, ordinarily will have grown quite weary of having to carry the load that should have been borne by others.

Thus, when the new owner steps forth purposefully to purge the acquired firm of weak people, he or she customarily meets with the approval of the real contributors. In fact, this should serve as a motivating event for contributors. It is related to the fourth reason for expeditiously terminating the incumbents who haven't been measuring up as they should. Specifically, when lackluster performers are let go, that opens up slots that allow the promotion and reassignment of more promising personnel. This kind of housecleaning and reallocation of human resources is particularly appropriate in the merger/acquisition arena where people are expecting change.

Opportunities for Streamlining

Top management in the acquiring firm usually finds that just as there is a need to get rid of insurgents, redundant personnel, and nonperformers, there is also some fat that can be trimmed. Practically all organizations accrue a certain amount of excess baggage as years go by. It's an insidious process, and something to which the target company grows accustomed. But the sharp eye of the acquirer should be able to ascertain where these opportunities for streamlining exist.

There may be people in the management ranks who are a manifestation of the Peter Principle—people who have "reached their level of incompetence" and are quite expendable. Perhaps in being kicked upstairs they have been made relatively harmless. But if they are in over their heads, and particularly if they are rather nonproductive, they should be viewed as candidates for termination. Again, the vacancies created may provide superb opportunities to promote up-and-comers who can revitalize the acquired firm.

There may be others on board who, though quite capable and even reasonably productive, have been given make-shift assignments that fall short of justifying their continuing existence on the company roster. Some of these folks may be worthy of reassignment or transfer, but at the very least their work role should be scrutinized and their contribution carefully weighed. If these people cannot be channeled along more productive paths, they, too, should be dismissed.

Other incumbents may be identified who have ended up in assignments for which they are poorly cast. The postmerger environment can be an opportune time to correct these unsuitable appointments that have been tolerated too long. Some of these mismatches may indeed involve high-caliber talent that could be most beneficial to the acquired (or parent) firm if the people were reassigned. But this calls for careful assessment of the person as well as the organization's needs, an appraisal process that should occur early in the postmerger scheme of things. If it is determined that these personnel are expendable, in all likelihood the ties should be severed as part of a global, systematic effort to make the acquired firm more lean and trim.

PEOPLE RECRUITED AWAY FROM THE FIRM

When word begins to circulate that a company has been targeted for acquisition, it often pricks up the ears of corporate recruiters and executive search consultants. They know, at least implicitly, that the event will increase the likelihood that people within the firm to be acquired will be more approachable than before. The situation is viewed as "open season," one of the easiest times to lure away technical specialists, key managers, and executives.

Mergers and acquisitions generally cause people to reassess their careers, examine their alternatives, and check out promising options.

In other words, they become much more amenable to putting themselves on the market, whereas under normal circumstances they might prefer to remain settled, steadfast, and secure in their jobs. These employees may not have looked at the employment ads for many years. Ordinarily, they might be inclined to dismiss any overtures another potential employer might send their way. But being acquired changes all that.

High-talent people, in particular, will often opt for immediate guarantees they can negotiate with a new employer rather than wait out the merger situation and gamble that their careers will be well served (or at least not damaged) by the acquisition of their firm. This is especially true when the parent organization has a bad reputation in the business world for its handling of acquisitions.

Those who are recruited away might never have become bailouts, much less terminations, but they still can become a part of management turnover statistics. When they leave, ordinarily they not only weaken the company but also frequently end up strengthening the competition that has stepped in to take advantage of the situation.

CHAPTER 5

The Need for a Comprehensive Appraisal of the Acquired Company's Key Talent

Over the years, the conventional practice of making staffing changes on the heels of an acquisition has taken one of two forms. Sometimes the acquired firm steps in early to make people changes, whether in just a handful of positions or with wholesale reorganization. In the other approach, the parent company attempts to maintain a hands-off stance—again, except for perhaps one or two initial changes—until several months have elapsed that hopefully allow enough time for everyone to calm down and become adjusted to the situation. One of the familiar steps in this second tactic involves assurances from executives in the parent company to the effect that, "We don't plan any personnel changes."

In both of these approaches, however, the critical element that's missing is a systematic, incisive assessment of what the acquisition brings vis-à-vis management and technical talent. Typically, the acquiring firm will take a piecemeal approach, wherein a few people here and there are evaluated in a professional fashion. Or a number of people may be appraised in a sketchy manner but so superficially that much room remains for potential problems to develop.

Top management in the acquiring firm might argue that it is best to allow some time for it to get to know the abilities and potentials of the management team in the target organization. But that assumes that those people will hang around long enough for such a familiarization process to occur. Often they do not. Furthermore, if the slow route is taken, a part of this getting-acquainted exercise may consist of seeing bad management decisions being made, mistakes that could have been prevented. Likewise, key opportunities may be lost. All in all, this can prove to be an expensive and time-consuming education process. This approach also drags out the integration of the two firms. It forestalls needed resolution and leaves questions unanswered, prolonging the anxiety and ambiguity, thus contributing to the chronic problem of postmerger drift.

This approach is not necessarily a kind and thoughtful way of dealing with staffing matters. Nor is it likely to be viewed favorably by people in the acquired organization. Rather than looking on this as a fair and equitable opportunity to prove themselves, they will more likely be anxiously waiting to see when and where the axe will fall.

The situation feels like benign neglect to people in the acquisition, as if they are being left to dangle helplessly in the wind. In their opinion, it would be better to get closure, to be appraised promptly and fairly, so that they can get on with their careers either secure in the merged firm or somewhere else.

WHY SHOULD INCUMBENTS BE EVALUATED?

It might be argued that in several merger scenarios it is best to go with the status quo—that is, move on the premise that the incumbent management team is sound and that the acquiring company should not fool around with something that's working. This line of reasoning sounds good on the surface, especially if the acquired firm is financially healthy and has a pretty good track record. Upon careful scrutiny, however, it proves to be flawed in a number of respects.

Some Incumbents May Not Play to Stay To begin with, the acquirer needs to ascertain who plans to remain on board. The new owner may be extremely fond of the new charges and fully confident that they can continue to operate the company in a successful fashion. But that's no guarantee whatsoever that the feelings are reciprocal. Even if these incumbents are not grumbling, even if they appear to be reconciled to the situation, in-depth data gathering often proves otherwise. The acquirer should rapidly identify fast-track, high-talent employees so that the parent company can put forth special efforts to retain them. Often these people can be "hooked" with heavy-duty assignments and special developmental opportunities that clearly communicate the key role they can play in the organization's future.

It is particularly important for the new owner to take pains to identify these people and tie them to the organization if the acquisition represents a move by the parent company into new terrain, for example, unfamiliar products/services and different markets. The less one understands the business that has been bought, the more crucial it is to keep those people on board who do have a firm grasp of what it takes to make the business a success. The same general idea holds true, of course, if the acquirer does not have any surplus management talent to speak of that could be sent across to manage things in the event key vacancies develop in the acquisition. And after an adversative merger battle has been fought, as in a raid or contested situation, the question of who is willing to stay is a particularly sensitive issue.

Some People Should Be Repositioned or Terminated Virtually any management team has a weak link here or there. And the odds are that even a successful company can work better if the weaker performers are identified. This does not mean that they will always be replaced. But parent company executives can determine how best to maneuver around a person's shortcomings through the use of support personnel, changing certain features of the job itself, or focusing on developing the incumbent's skills. At any rate, the parent company can be well served by identifying management vulnerabilities early on. It can preempt many nasty, costly surprises by giving the parent firm an opportunity to take preventive measures.

Also, if the merger has brought about departmental overlap or duplicated functions, and the integration game plan calls for keeping only one person in those situations, an early evaluation will indicate which person should be groomed to fill the opening.

Data for Management Succession Planning   The acquirer needs to know where promotion potential exists in order for good management succession planning to take place. There is virtually always some early turnover in key management positions, and decisions must be made regarding promotions, transfers, and recruitment of new blood. A broad-gauged management assessment develops the kind of database necessary to move decisively in those situations.

Executives in the parent company can benefit from having an accurate "fix" on people's limits plus their potential for shouldering heavier duties or altogether different types of assignments. The merger/acquisition arena is no place for trial-and-error staffing decisions.

Learn How to Manage and Motivate   By getting a quick, comprehensive set of insights into the makeup of the management corps in the acquired company, the parent firm possesses the information needed to best manage and motivate these people from day one.

Ordinarily, it will be found that some of the acquired personnel need generous job structure—that is, clear-cut marching orders, very specific objectives, and definitive procedural guidelines. Others will operate best in an environment where they are given very free rein and generous latitude to exercise their own judgment. Some people are best motivated by attention, approval, and hand-holding. Others will perform best under a strict boss who is quick to discipline.

The key point here is that it is very easy to mismanage, and therein demotivate, people you don't know. It also is extremely easy to violate the practices people have grown accustomed to over the years. When that happens, the odds are significantly increased that bailouts will occur, that people will be recruited away more easily, or at least that their job performance will deteriorate.

Identify Training Needs   Some people—even some of the best talent—need additional training to measure up to the new demands they will encounter. Keep in mind that it is just as likely as not that these people will prefer to keep quiet about the struggle they are having. They will be unaccustomed to asking for help. This suggests, then, that the acquirer needs to be highly sensitive to where incumbent personnel will in all likelihood need training or coaching.

Opportunity for Coaching and Management Development   Since mergers and acquisitions produce so much dissonance, since they are such a destabilizing force, they typically act as an "unfreezing" event for employees. People are jarred out of their familiar routines. There is a significant increase in introspection, leading managers and others to examine themselves and their modus operandi.

This mental state makes them far more receptive to the idea of behavior change or efforts aimed toward self-improvement. Thus, on the heels of an acquisition, the timing is right for management-development activities.

A careful, thorough evaluation in this atmosphere produces data that can be shared with an incumbent in a very meaningful feedback session. With receptivity to personal change being at a peak, constructive coaching is far more likely to produce desired behavior change than it would in ordinary circumstances.

Assessing Adaptability   Some people who did well under the old regime will not be able to adapt to the new setup. For example, the new system may not tolerate or indulge their shortcomings and idiosyncrasies.

The company may be moving out of a fast-growth mode into a stabilization period, and this may call for more of a "maintenance manager." Or it may be that in the months ahead the company will need high-powered marketing savvy more than the financial expertise an incumbent has. A person who did well in a more structured, premerger environment may now be surpassed by someone who fared poorly in that world but has the capacity to shine in the current climate of ambiguity.

A systematic appraisal process may well identify which people are likely to become weak performers, passive resisters, or even clear-cut insurgents. It is ironic that usually some of the best people in the acquired company adapt most slowly to the postmerger requirements. This seems to occur because strong performers typically are very committed to their own style and pursue their own priorities with such conviction.

Measuring Motivation   Executives, previously highly driven performers, may lose much of their motivation if the merger makes them independently wealthy. Their commitment may drop, with a resulting sag in their day-to-day performance. Entrepreneurial spirit, initiative, and resource-fulness frequently deteriorate in key players once they are cloaked in financial security. There are also other merger dynamics at work to compound the problem: loss of clear role identity, the fact that ultimate fiscal responsibility rests with someone else, less feeling of ownership, a drop in independent authority, and so on.

The owner/entrepreneur, in particular, is prone to feel rather inhibited if he or she remains to operate in the post-merger setting. People such as this are not accustomed to having to answer to anyone. Now, with skilled and rather sophisticated executives there to second-guess and require adherence to a new management style and unfamiliar per-formance measures, the owner/entrepreneur often becomes anxious. There is an overwhelming fear of being seen as inept. Those who are not insecure may become demotivated out of aggravation. An in-house merger/acquisition paper at Westinghouse submits that few owner/managers are, in fact, worth to the business what it would take to fully moti-vate them toward long-term, high-level performance on be-half of "their" business. A higher percentage of Westing-house acquisitions should be accompanied by the planned replacement of top management of the acquired company either immediately or after a short transition period.

So a thorough assessment is serviceable here in two respects: First, in anticipating which personnel are likely to slacken off and, second, in providing the parent company with insight into the trials facing the owner/entrepreneur. The essential point is that incumbents cannot be adequately evaluated strictly on the basis of history or past performance. Rather, they must be measured against the future in terms of what it brings by way of goals to be accomplished and problems to be overcome.

What Really Accounts for the Company's Track Record?   The company's past success may be due primarily

to factors other than abilities and efforts of incumbent management. A broad-gauged management assessment can give valuable clues regarding this sort of situation.

The same thing is true, of course, in the other direction. A firm that is courting bankruptcy is not always devoid of competent managers and executives. There may well be bonafide winners in the crowd somewhere. If so, they should prove most valuable in helping the acquirer achieve a turnaround, assuming they can be identified and retained.

WHY NOT EVALUATE THE ACQUIRED COMPANY'S MANAGEMENT ON THE BASIS OF CORPORATE GROWTH AND PROFITABILITY?

This is the most traditional approach, and it is good so far as it goes. Certainly, it does pay respect to salient—even critical—data. But good numbers can mask weak talent. The acquired company may for all practical purposes have been a one-man show. There may be no backup. That in itself is bad enough, but it becomes even more critical if the front man happens to depart in the aftermath of the acquisition.

There are too many external biasing factors that deserve consideration for the parent company to simply assume that incumbents truly deserve full credit for the current set of numbers. A quantitative analysis can be misleading in a variety of ways.

A Product of Good Times   A benevolent economy may deserve most of the credit for the acquired firm's good financial performance. So the question that deserves thought is whether there is much proof that incumbents can manage a down economy or a postmerger situation successfully.

Short-Term Perspective   Management may be guilty of mortgaging the future to achieve short-term results. Statistics that look good today may have been achieved at tomorrow's expense. For example, the financial ledger may look good because there has been no money spent on R&D, capital improvements, and so on. The workforce may have been slashed to cut overhead, but this may have been done at the expense of adequate servicing of the company's products. And, given time, these sorts of executive decisions could conceivably prove devastating to the firm. Numbers that look good on the surface may actually be fragile evidence of executive talent. Management may have built a house of cards that faces a shaky, uncertain future.

The Hand of Fate   Pure luck may have been on the company's side. Chance timing may deserve most of the credit, as management simply may have stumbled into good fortune. Or a foolish gamble may have worked although it never should have been taken.

The trend that has buoyed the financial picture may be about to reverse—for example, a fast-growth strategy may be on the brink of corporate wreckage, with financial resources overextended and management capacities strained beyond reason.

Undeserved Credit?   It is possible that good numbers result primarily from the backup strength given by managers or technically skilled individuals who have already left the firm or who probably will leave. Likewise, managers or technical people may have been in slots where their own effectiveness has been masked by the strong or weak performance of another person.

In other words, who really owns the statistics? Who is primarily responsible for the acquired firm's present financial status? Who has taken up the slack for whom?

A Race with Only One Runner   A quantitatively favorable picture may be the result of little or no competition. And that, of course, can conceivably change. So long as one has the only grocery store in town, the numbers may look pretty good, but they may say very little about managerial competence. It is interesting to observe how many major corporations appeared to be well managed until they were confronted with stiff competition from Japanese imports in the form of automobiles, steel, and electronics.

Environmental Forces Changing markets and changing access to raw materials due to political/governmental forces may cause top management to have numbers that look particularly good or bad. For example, price supports, deregulation, import tariffs, weather, or even war are external forces that can bias a company's financial picture dramatically without making any valid statement about the caliber of the management team.

False Statistics Numbers often lie. And they are often manipulated to make top management look better than it should. For example, the way inventories and facilities are valued, the tax angles that are played, and other accounting shenanigans can present a very misleading picture regarding top management's true track record.

In his book *How to Measure Managerial Performance*, Richard Sloma states:

> Output from the accounting system, while perfectly acceptable to the public audit firm, may be not only useless to a management performance measurement program, but actually counterproductive, in that management performance may be inaccurately measured. The "best" array of measures always includes a "blend" of data, from both outside and within the accounting system.[1]

How versus How Much Qualitative issues or factors may be more important than quantitative measures. For instance, an executive's ethics, strategic vision, human relations skills, and so on may deserve more consideration than the numbers he or she can boast. Perhaps the executive swung a $50 million deal by making a $50,000 bribe or achieved impressive market share by stealing trade secrets. It might be that the CEO has an adversarial manner that has enabled him or her to aggressively generate some good financial results thus far but that will eventually precipitate a strike or lawsuit. In short, you can't separate the ends from the means.

But all too often, the leaders of an acquired firm are appraised on the basis of quantitative data, the profits, or the bottom line, what the company has shown vis-à-vis earnings, stock prices, and growth in revenues. Parent company executives need to scrutinize the *qualitative* data on its acquired management team, as this information represents part of the "hidden economics" of the deal.

WHAT'S WRONG WITH LETTING INCUMBENT EXECUTIVES IN THE TARGET COMPANY SUBMIT AN APPRAISAL OF THEIR OWN MANAGEMENT TEAM?

Take what the president, CEO, or owner has to offer, but don't take for granted that the acquired firm can give you an accurate, unbiased appraisal of its own incumbent managers. The people mentioned may not be able to and may not want to. Usually, the data they supply can be extremely helpful. But they are far from being a sufficiently thorough, reliable critique.

Usually the top-ranking individual gives an off-the-cuff evaluation of key people in the firm, if there is a critique given at all. On one hand, it's astounding that acquirers are no more consistent than they are in using this person as a source for these data. But it is also amazing that some acquirers are so ready to take at face value what this person might say about subordinates. There are myriad reasons for questioning the validity and completeness of this person's critique of management and other personnel in the acquisition. Imagine a situation in which the person involved in negotiating the sale of a company has been asked by the acquirer to evaluate some of his or her key people.

Parting Gestures   This may be the senior executive's best (perhaps last) chance to repay old debts to incumbents. Thus, it is almost certain that he or she will feel certain obligations to defend them. If the owner has sold the organization and plans to leave the picture, that person will want to be remembered fondly. The executive may also suffer pangs of guilt as a result of having sold the company, and in attempting to assuage these feelings, may allow a positive bias to creep into the management critique.

The Last to Know   It is not uncommon to find that the owner or CEO is actually somewhat out of touch with the people and their plans. It might be, for example, that a couple of key executives are on the verge of leaving to start a competing firm. The top executive almost always fails to maintain an accurate feel for the pulse of the organization when much of his or her time and energies are directed at finding a buyer, negotiating a sale, or perhaps trying to fend off a corporate raider.

Promoting the In-Crowd   The key executive who plans to remain in an active role with the firm may strive—even unconsciously—to entrench loyal supporters and thereby retain a power base. It is extremely difficult to be objective, not protective, of one's own advocates or constituency.

Wrong Perspective   The acquired company's top executive may not really grasp what the firm will need by way of management talent in the postmerger situation. He or she may not know where the buyer plans to go with the new acquisition. Unless this executive is really on the right wavelength, the appraisal of subordinates vis-à-vis the new corporate future will be unreliable.

Blind Spots   The owner or key executive in the acquired firm simply may not be a very good judge of talent and ability. He or she may attribute success to the wrong people, such as lauding the vice president of sales for the firm's revenues instead of crediting some outstanding sales managers who actually managed to achieve the excellent sales volumes in spite of the vice president of sales. It is common to find top executives overrating certain traits or factors while underrating the importance of others. For example, a man who doesn't like subordinates who challenge him will often view aggressiveness as a negative attribute, when it might be a highly sought characteristic by management in the parent organization.

Pride of Ownership   There is a vested interest on the part of the senior executive who proceeds to critique the strengths and weaknesses of subordinates. After all, this is the person responsible for putting the team together in the first place. In evaluating the management team negatively, the executive would essentially be criticizing his or her own performance. It is very difficult to do that without pulling punches.

Blackball   It may be that a person in the acquired company with real talent has been blacklisted along the way somehow, and thus may not be evaluated justly by superiors.

No Bearer of Bad News   The acquired company's top officer may say what sounds good instead of laying cold, hard, and unwelcome facts on the line.

Remember, this is the company that the owner or CEO has been trying to sell, and undoubtedly has been presenting in the most favorable light. This person has probably been singing its praises—highlighting its good points—while downplaying, ignoring, or even concealing its flaws and vulnerabilities. It could take months to find out just how weak some acquired managers are, and by then the damage is usually already done: Opportunities have been lost, accounts have been bungled, and so on.

Familiar Words, Different Meanings The key executive in the acquisition probably does not know the parent company well enough to evaluate people from that frame of reference. Parent company norms may be quite different regarding what is seen as good, what is mediocre, and what is weak.

The standards and the semantics can vary dramatically from one company to another, particularly if the companies are in different industries and are of widely divergent sizes.

Charges of Bias from People in the Acquiring Firm People in the parent company may not accept the critique as a fair, objective appraisal. Moreover, they probably shouldn't, for the very reasons mentioned above. The more there is to be a true merger of the two organizations, the more this becomes a problem of real significance. If managers or technical personnel from the two companies will be vying for the same slots, a more objective, nonpartisan means of appraising candidates needs to be arranged.

Who's Outside the Inner Circle? People at the acquired company may wish for an external, objective evaluation that precludes cronyism, nepotism, or other means of playing favorites. Even if the parent company does happen to be comfortable with the idea that the acquisition's owner or CEO can provide an adequate and equitable appraisal of incumbent managers, some of the people working there may not be comfortable with the idea at all. Furthermore, they may have very good reasons for feeling that way.

Will History Repeat Itself?   Finally, it could well be that some incumbents in the acquired firm will do things (or have done things) for the "old man" they would never do for the parent company—for example, make personal sacrifices or exhibit unusual commitment. The very same people, under the new parent company's influence and management, may give an altogether different performance. It may be worse; it may be better. Either way, the "old man's" appraisal of these people may be a very accurate description of what he has experienced in the relationship, but it may not be duplicated under the new regime.

WHAT'S WRONG WITH HAVING SOME EXECUTIVES IN THE ACQUIRING COMPANY MAKE A CASUAL, SUBTLE, INFORMAL ASSESSMENT OF THE TARGET COMPANY'S MANAGEMENT TEAM?

Again, nothing is wrong so long as this approach is not overrated. This can provide a particularly important assessment on some technical matters and "personal chemistry" issues.

Still, there are a variety of problems in relying on this means of determining the strengths and weaknesses of the acquired firm's human resources.

Questionable Objectivity   Some of the executives in the parent company may have something to lose. They may have an axe to grind so that they cannot be sufficiently objective. Often, this is an unconscious bias, but very pernicious just the same.

It is conceivable that a particularly high-powered, ambitious individual in the target company poses a bit of a threat to one of the acquirer's executives, who envisions the possibility that they could both be vying for the same position some day in the not too distant future. Or perhaps the parent company executive has been mentoring someone in his own organization who must now compete with this talented newcomer.

Sometimes the bias grows out of the unstated assumption that, "We're the buyer, that must mean we're better." This mental syndrome frequently pervades the parent company, adds to the polarization of the two firms, and contributes to unfair comparisons of people.

Evaluate the Evaluator So much of the time, this sort of appraisal exercise does not play to the strengths of the parent company executives who are involved in the process. They may give it their best shot, and even do a respectable job, but the odds are it does not represent their real forte. This evaluation remains a crucial task, however, and should be conducted in as professional a manner as possible.

Shooting from the Hip A casual, informal evaluation is just not sufficient. Too much is at stake to take a haphazard, unsystematic approach to appraising the competencies of key people in the acquired firm. But the evaluation is almost always an unstructured exercise when it is being done by parent company executives. Ordinarily, these executives sort of play it by ear, leaning much too heavily on "gut feel," inconsistent measures, and incomplete data.

Other Priorities Usually, parent company executives have their hands full doing other things. For them to become heavily involved in this appraisal process pulls them away from tasks where their best abilities likely can be better employed. And the very fact that they are busy and preoccupied with other priorities increases the odds that this task will be shortchanged in terms of the time and effort it receives.

Lowering the Trust Level   If it is very apparent that, in fact, they are being evaluated by the parent company, the incumbents in the acquisition will probably be more guarded and defensive than they would be if they were being evaluated by an outsider. The people under consideration are far more likely to open up and share feelings and perceptions if the evaluation is conducted by someone who can bring objectivity as well as professionalism to the task. Furthermore, incumbents are almost certain to view this evaluation as a more fair and equitable assessment of their abilities and potential.

WHY NOT CLEAN HOUSE?

Sometimes, the acquirer elects to make wholesale changes. Rather than go through the exercise of having anyone do much of an assessment of incumbents, they are unilaterally dismissed and—in those positions deemed necessary for continued company operations—replaced with new recruits or with transfers from the parent company.

This may appear to be the line of least resistance, but that appearance probably is deceiving. Even when an acquisition involves rescuing a company from insolvency, there is a more prudent way to deal with staffing decisions and management succession planning. The problems are manifold in deciding to clean house.

Salvage What You Can   Housecleaning probably means throwing out the good with the bad. Somewhere in the management and technical ranks, there is bound to be some valuable talent that should be retained.

Bridging the Gap   Housecleaning sacrifices people who possess a valuable sense of history about the company and who can give your corporate effort an important element of continuity. In their absence, the transition period is likely to be significantly prolonged.

The parent company invariably will find that the acquired firm suffers a severe loss of momentum during the restaffing process. The postmerger dip in productivity is almost always an inescapable problem, but while it cannot be avoided completely, it certainly can be minimalized. It is compounded, however, when there is a broad-ranging purge of existing personnel.

Intangible Assets   The acquirer loses whatever is "in people's heads" regarding operations, products, the competition, and so on. In virtually any organization, there are undeveloped ideas and programs that have substantial value but that have not been put in writing or another form of permanent record. Important data regarding how business is conducted have not been captured in any book of procedures or operating guidelines. Incumbents succeed in dealing with certain clients because of the intimate insights that have been developed over time, but this is carried with them when they leave. These intangibles can never be fully retrieved.

Polarization   Cleaning house threatens and alienates the remaining workforce, fostering a highly adversarial climate. Furthermore, because of the extremely adverse impact cleaning house has on trust, behavior is driven underground and the communication networks take a long time to recover. Overall, the event has a strong inhibiting influence on those employees who remain. At the very time the acquirer needs the most from these people, they become much more cautious and self-protective as they go about their duties.

Damaged Business Relationships As part of the housecleaning, the parent company risks the loss of key contacts that have been developed over the years. The ties that have been forged with political and civic leaders, customers, or even suppliers are commonly based on personal friendships. These important outsiders are often offended by the way their friends have been treated by the new owner and therefore seek their own vengeance. Key accounts may go elsewhere, and it may become much more difficult to negotiate with vendors. Power brokers in the business community or the government sector can create innumerable obstacles that otherwise would never have developed.

Wasted Efforts The housecleaning approach ordinarily derails valuable projects or programs that are in progress but that are not far enough along to survive on their own. This could include research efforts, marketing plans, new product development, and training or other personnel programs.

Demotivation Wholesale terminations are usually devastating to morale in the acquired firm as the employees see their organization being dismembered. Job commitment and company loyalty fizzle. Thus, intangible motivating forces that may have been important components of the firm's previous success no longer exist. Key facets of the underlying corporate culture are dislodged, resulting in a more apathetic workforce that is unresponsive to the new owner's attempts to rally and regroup those employees who remain.

Stiffening the Opposition The housecleaning approach chases incumbents over to the competitor's house, where their knowledge can be quite damaging to the parent company. Not only do they take their talents to the opposition, they go with a vindictive spirit. So the acquirer ends up with new enemies both within and without.

A Troublesome Reputation Housecleaning gives rise to an image of the parent company as a ruthless acquirer. Obviously, this label can plague the new owner in any subsequent acquisition efforts. Most companies are very leery of talking merger with a firm that has developed this kind of reputation. Even when subsequent deals are struck and the acquirer has no intention of being "the new broom that sweeps clean," people in the target firm will be running scared because of the parent company's notoriety.

A Dollar Drain If some of the incumbent managers or executives have arranged golden parachutes for themselves, housecleaning can become a very costly approach from a purely monetary standpoint. Finally, restaffing can become an expensive exercise in and of itself. Executives' time spent in courting, interviewing, and orienting replacement personnel adds up in a hurry.

Wrap-Up Points To sum up, there are several admonitions the parent company should consider. First, the new owner should not be tempted to "go with the familiar person." This tactic does not sufficiently minimize the risks involved.

Second, there is real danger in deciding to "Do nothing and wait for the dust to settle." It may, on the surface, appear that in employing this approach one is exercising sage restraint. But some good people may choose to leave while the merger is still stirring up dust. Others will have been waffling along with a wait-and-see attitude. And some will have done damage that could have been prevented by a more timely termination or reassignment. Undoubtedly, the organization will have lost some momentum unnecessarily while also wasting an excellent opportunity to motivate people.

Third, sweeping personnel changes that follow closely on the heels of an acquisition, and which proceed without any systematic appraisal of those people being terminated, come at too dear a cost.

CHAPTER 6

A Three-Way Evaluation of Managerial and Technical Talent

A systematic appraisal of significant personnel in an acquisition calls for input from several directions. A multifaceted approach generates a database that is most useful because it is (1) more accurate and (2) more informative than any appraisal growing out of a single data source.

The first and most obvious appraisal of incumbents should draw on the insights of the owner and/or senior executive in the acquired firm. The second stage in the three-way process should be an objective, professional evaluation conducted by a management/organizational psychologist. The third data input should consist of the perceptions of executives in the acquiring organization. When the three sets of data are blended, a very serviceable composite picture should emerge of each of the key people in the acquired firm.

INPUT FROM THE ACQUIRED FIRM'S OWNER OR CEO

The dangers of relying too heavily on this data input have already been highlighted. Nevertheless, it does remain a logical point of inquiry vis-à-vis the abilities, potentials, attitudes, and orientations of incumbents.

What is needed, and what is usually not employed, is a systematic and consistent format for this senior executive to follow in sharing his or her thoughts about subordinates. Ideally, it will take the form of a structured interview conducted by another person—for example, a management/ organizational psychologist or perhaps a senior manager in the parent company's personnel department. This third party conducts the interview, adhering to the structured format and thus ensuring that all incumbents are appraised with the same level of thoroughness and according to the same sort of rating criteria.

Invariably, there is a fund of rich data in the key executive's head; it is the job of the third party to elicit, organize, and interpret it appropriately. The owner or CEO is in a position to evaluate subordinates in the context of the company he or she knows better than anyone else. As this person probably has the best grasp of make-or-break traits and talents, too, incumbents will be appraised on highly relevant behavior or characteristics. Ordinarily, this senior executive can readily cite a number of "critical incidents" that substantiate the assessment.

The third party conducting the interview plays another key role: helping the senior executive past his or her own personal biases. This permits the pros and cons to be weighed more dispassionately.

A side benefit of these interviews is that the third party will invariably glean critically valuable insights into the acquired firm's organizational culture or personality, operating style, predominant managerial philosophy, and overall company norms. These insights can be most valuable in subsequent efforts to facilitate integration of the two companies.

The third party should have the top executive critique the key managers and technical specialists by structuring an analysis of these incumbents individually on the following points:

- Major strengths.
- Weaker points or shortcomings.
- How this person compensates, or what accounts most for his or her job effectiveness.
- Record of achieving goals and objectives.
- Major accomplishments / contributions.
- Major mistakes / problems in past performance.
- Management style.
- Most common management mistakes.
- Environment in which the person works best (and worst).
- Transferability to other job assignments or management responsibilities.
- Where the person needs backup and support.
- Problems in managing the individual.
- How the person can best be motivated.
- Next logical career step.
- Long-range potential.
- Developmental needs.

Having accomplished this, the third party should then pursue a line of questioning designed to get a better feel for how the employee is likely to react to the merger / acquisition. Here, the inquiry should address such topics as the following:

- How the person will react to the merger / acquisition. What he or she stands to gain.
- What the person stands to lose.
- Likelihood that the employee will stay with the company (including specific forces that would persuade the person to stay and how to increase these and thereby tie him or her to the firm, if that is what is desired).
- Specific forces that would be an influence in leaving (including how to increase these or eliminate them, as appropriate).

- Problems / risks—or benefits—of the person leaving (including impact on other people and how this might influence them to leave also, and critical roles the individual plays in the organization's social system).
- Who, if anyone, should or could replace this person if he or she leaves.
- How well the person will adapt to the parent company's management philosophy and operating style.
- Key backers or advocates this person has in the firm. His or her adversaries in the acquired firm.
- Personal idiosyncrasies.
- Questions or concerns the owner or CEO has regarding this individual.

This key executive might be asked, in closing, for any additional conclusions or recommendations that would affect the disposition of the incumbent in the postmerger environment. Finally, it can be helpful to have this top executive in the acquired firm place each of the key subordinates in one of the following categories:

- Should be separated from the company.
- Questionable need to keep with the company.
- Not critical whether the employee leaves or remains.
- Efforts should be made to keep the employee with the company.
- Critical to retain.

EVALUATION BY AN OUTSIDE PROFESSIONAL

Step two in the three-pronged approach to evaluating key incumbents consists of an in-depth appraisal by an outside professional, someone who has the unique tools as well as the objectivity needed to add an important dimension to this audit of the acquired human resources. This might be a management psychologist, executive recruiter, or some human resource specialist skilled in assessment techniques.

Ordinarily, this appraiser will conduct a thorough background interview with each person and possibly do testing. As part of the face-to-face inquiry, the appraiser should delve into such areas as the incumbent's career objectives and feelings regarding the merger. Specifically, the individual being evaluated should be given the opportunity to speak at some length about his or her feelings concerning the parent company, fears and concerns relative to the acquisition, and so on.

This exercise is sometimes threatening to those who are asked to participate, and for that reason they might be given the opportunity for a "feedback session" with the professional responsible for gathering and interpreting the data. This second meeting is most likely to occur several days or weeks later. It provides the person being evaluated another chance to open up and freely ventilate feelings and opinions about the corporate marriage. Frequently, this allows data to surface regarding how the merger is being perceived or how the parent company might take steps to overcome problems that are developing.

The people who are asked to participate in the professional evaluation may be a little uneasy, somewhat wary about it all. But they also are inclined to view it as a noteworthy effort on the part of the acquirer to deal with people in the purchased firm in an equitable, informed fashion. Most people will open up and talk much more freely with an outsider than with parent company executives, particularly if this third party displays a good grasp of merger dynamics. Almost always, the key people in the acquisition appreciate the opportunity to tell their story, to make a pitch for themselves. Furthermore, if arrangements are made for individual follow-up sessions to go over the data, participants may get a once-in-a-lifetime chance to hear a professional advise them in a supportive, insightful manner on matters such as these:

- How strengths can be played to most effectively.
- How weaker points can be compensated for, maneuvered around, or perhaps overcome completely.
- What developmental steps could contribute most to career effectiveness.
- What changes the merger/acquisition may call for in terms of management style or work habits.
- What job opportunities it would be most appropriate to seek in the new corporate setup and which ones would carry a high potential for failure.

Parent company executives, in turn, get a quick and thorough feel for what they have acquired in terms of managerial and technical resources in the acquired firm. Management succession planning can thus proceed more promptly and in a far more sophisticated, strategic fashion. The professional evaluation eliminates the need for much guesswork as the new owner goes about making staffing decisions. Moreover, in the months that follow, far fewer unpleasant surprises crop up because people in the acquired firm were initially misread, misunderstood, and miscast.

EVALUATION OF KEY PERSONNEL IN THE ACQUIRED FIRM BY COMPANY EXECUTIVES

Top management in the acquiring organization should be involved in the third aspect of the appraisal process. In this exercise, top management should meet with those responsible for carrying out the assessments in steps one and two. Here, in joint session, the objective is to pool insights, weigh the ramifications of the data, and draw final conclusions regarding the disposition of those personnel who are under review.

Parent company executives play a key role in this stage of the three-way evaluation. Their responsibility is to critique the key people in the acquisition on a number of crucial factors—for example, personal chemistry, technical skills, operating style, and corporate culture.

It may be that the top executive in the acquired firm gives particularly good marks to one of those directly reporting to him. Likewise, the professional appraiser may submit data endorsing the idea that the person is, in fact, just as strong and capable as the superior indicated. But if senior management in the parent organization has experienced a personality conflict in meeting and interacting with this particular person, there may be little hope of a compatible working relationship. It could also be, however, that the other two data inputs, plus the facilitative influence of the outside appraiser, enhance the parent company's understanding of and respect for the individual in question. And instead of a highly promising person being terminated or allowed to bail out because of interpersonal friction with the new owner, a mutually rewarding relationship may be allowed to evolve.

When inputs from all three stages of the evaluation converge, accurate and serviceable answers are found to the questions of "Who should go?" "Who will (and should) stay?" and "How can those people who do stay best be managed and motivated for the success of the merged organization?"

CHAPTER 7

Protecting the Investment through Rerecruitment

Organizations have a hard enough time hanging on to good talent these days. Careers have become more a collection of assignments than a collection of seniority pins and gold watches. Work has come to be seen as more an activity than a place. Because of this, the feeling of company belonging and loyalty is a rarer experience than when 20-year stints at the patriarchal corporation were the norm. Introduce a destablizing event like a merger or acquisition into the picture, and the precarious ties holding employees in their current jobs begin to loosen even further.

The nature of today's deals makes this erosion of loyalty still more of an issue. So many of today's mergers and acquisitions are not really based on the idea of purchasing hard assets such as plants and equipment. Due to the growth of the service industry, the deemphasis of leveraged buyouts, and the increase in the value of knowledge, a large percentage of today's purchases and consolidations represent a pursuit of "soft assets." These soft assets represent the knowledge of the workforce in the target company—for example, the value of patents, relationships with clients, and the opportunities that lie ahead because of the expertise surrounding new products and services under development. Many of today's deals are attractive financial propositions solely because of the knowledge of the people in the company being acquired.

What can be done to protect the investment in this sort of merger or acquisition? One key answer is to conduct a rapid, well-organized, and persuasive rerecruitment effort aimed at the key talent you want to retain.

WHY PEOPLE LEAVE

It is not surprising that people often choose to leave an organization or "decommit" during a merger or acquisition. The widespread turmoil created by change turns people's thoughts inward, away from their job and toward personal concerns. Self-protective thoughts swirl through their minds, leaving people to wonder about the wisdom in waiting to see what will happen to their careers.

Remember, the first word in merger is *me*. For the time being, the big concerns people are wrestling with reflect their uncertainty about how they will fare in the new scheme of things. For example, they worry, "What will happen to *my* job, *my* pay, *my* security?" These doubts and unanswered questions create a great feeding ground for headhunters and company recruiters, who naturally step up their efforts to pick off the best talent. These recruiters who are circling the merger scene have the advantage of being able to buzz in fast and lay a hard offer in front of a person. This immediately provides the individual with an alternative to the ambiguity, uncertainty, and personal concerns he or she is experiencing.

The turnover statistics associated with mergers and acquisitions are staggering. Based on our data, when no coordinated retention actions are taken, 47 percent of all senior managers in an acquired firm leave within the first year of the acquisition. But the exodus doesn't stop there. Within the first three years, 72 percent end up heading for the door.

The costs associated with a talent drain of these pro-
portions are enormous. Perhaps equally damaging and just
as costly, though, are those people who stay on the payroll
but don't perform. They don't leave the company physi-
cally, but they emotionally check out. No longer feeling
any true commitment to their jobs or to the organization at
large, these people frequently join the ranks of the critics
and are resistive throughout the entire integration process.
In this instance, the organization ends up paying people to
cause problems.

RERECRUITMENT

One of the main challenges of the merger process is the
retention and revitalization of the valuable human capital
that is in place. This calls for a comprehensive and well-
planned rerecruitment strategy that proceeds with a strong
sense of urgency.

Three actions are particularly important in carrying out
this strategy. First, key people or groups must be identified.
Second, it is important to achieve an understanding of their
primary motivators. Finally, an action plan designed to address their motivators must be developed and implemented.
Such an approach should be executed with all the focus and
energy that are normally invested in finding new talent for
an organization. In a sense, that is exactly what is going on
here: A concentrated effort to persuade people and demonstrate to them that they should join the "new" organization.

Target the Key Talent

Earlier chapters describe in detail a systematic process for
evaluating personnel. That recommended approach—or
some variation of it—can identify the key people or groups
whose loss would have a detrimental impact on the success
of the business. Depending on the situation, people can be
considered important for various reasons. For the purposes

of this rerecruitment initiative, however, the "screen" to use in identifying your target personnel will be the consideration of whatever negative impact would come from losing them.

To proceed, then, make a list of the various people or groups and then determine how their leaving might damage the business. Would their departure also likely mean the loss of a key client or customer? Would it mean the loss of critical technical skills or maybe knowledge of a core product or service offering? When the answer indicates that losing a particular person would hurt, that individual should be considered a primary target for rerecruitment.

Many organizations have a documented succession plan that identifies the actions that would be taken to fill positions vacated by critical personnel. Although these plans are reactive in nature, they can serve as an excellent check to make sure that all the key people in the organization have been identified for rerecruitment efforts. The rerecruitment plan most likely will include everyone who is on the succession plan list, as well as additional people or groups.

Understand Their Motivators

Knowing what motivates a particular executive or employee is essential for effective rerecruitment. People vary greatly in terms of their personal needs, likes, and dislikes. Obviously, motivating angles can come from avoiding the dislikes as much as from addressing appetites. The following are items that might be important to people:

- ◆ **Security.** Based on the knowledge that one's job and career path have not been negatively affected by the merger.
- ◆ **Feeling "in."** A feeling of importance generated by allowing people to have input to, and knowledge of, decisions before they are widely announced.

- **Control.** At a time when feeling in control is uncommon, giving people options can make them feel valued as well as less vulnerable.
- **Ego items.** Those things that feed the ego and make one feel special are important to even the most pragmatic businesspeople.
- **Opportunity to "do the right thing."** Helping people understand the reasoning behind merger initiatives—sharing the "why"—appeals to people by helping them feel they are supporting the right approach.

The keener the insights into the individual, the better aimed your rerecruitment efforts can be. It is not necessarily the most expensive or most flamboyant motivator that gives you the most mileage in your efforts to retain someone. Above all, remember that it's a mistake to attribute to others your personal values or priorities regarding which motivators should count the most. The thing that would guarantee your willingness to stay on board might do nothing at all to keep the next person from leaving the organization.

Security When people think of organizational change, they often think of potential job loss. Job security, then, becomes a very basic issue to be reckoned with at all levels of an organization that is being acquired or merged. Obviously, the issue of job security needs to be addressed as promptly as possible for those employees who have been identified as critical to the company's future. Explain to them individually that they are each seen as someone who will play an important role and, as a result, will be kept in the organization. This communication should occur in private, and the message should be delivered in person. Acknowledge that the environment is uncertain at this early stage, and that there are many unknowns. But emphasize to these people that they are an integral part of making the changes work.

The second major aspect of security concerns financial matters. People will have all kinds of questions about their pay and benefits. Because money is such a fundamental concern in the minds of most people, rerecruitment can be a tough drill if you are not in a position to answer the dollar-related questions. The best situation, of course, is to be able to use pay raises, incentive contracts, and performance bonuses as part of the rerecruitment effort. But you often need to be rerecruiting before policies have been hammered out on compensation. In that case, consider "stay bonuses" as an interim means of assuring that the key people have the financial safety necessary to feel good about staying with the organization.

Feeling "In"   A basic need of people working in organizations is to feel "in" on things. They want to know what's going on. So one of the best ways to maintain the loyalty of key people during times of change is to keep them in the loop.

This can be accomplished in various ways, such as involving them in important meetings or sharing key information with them on a regular basis. Keep them posted about the alternatives being considered. Ask for their input. If these individuals are considered good enough to rerecruit, often they are good enough to help make the difficult decisions.

Some managers make the mistake of presuming they don't need to share information since no decisions have been made. But people feel more valued and more connected to the organization if they are kept informed.

Control   Over time, managers and executives develop a certain addiction to control. They want to enjoy a generous amount of influence over how things are handled. Many executives, in fact, develop a strong sense of self-worth relative to their span of control. During the merger-integration process, you can appeal to this need by leaving some decisions to them.

While it's true they might not handle things exactly the same way you would, there can be real benefits in allowing them to make the call. Granted, it may be necessary to set some boundaries around the decision-making process or to stress the need for communications about the decisions they're making. Beyond that, however, providing them latitude to make meaningful decisions can be a powerful motivator. This is particularly so in the merger/acquisition environment, where so many people in the management ranks are concerned about how they will be affected by the inevitable shakeup in the power balance.

Remember, too, that the effect of criticism is magnified during the transition period. Don't be too quick to criticize people for what looks like a bad decision. To the extent possible, reward people for acting quickly or taking accountability for making things happen. Then, as necessary, provide advice regarding how the decision could be made even more effectively the next time around.

Apart from satisfying managers' and executives' need for control, giving them decision-making latitude can help accelerate the integration process. They demonstrate more ownership of the desired changes, and show more initiative in the implementation of these changes.

Ego   Employee and management "work egos" operate on the belief that "I play an important role in the success of the organization." This belief gets fueled by a variety of things: a favorable self-concept, positive feedback from others, clear evidence of successful performance, and the status symbols provided to people in organizations. Ego plays a powerful role in how people feel about their employment. And in the merger/acquisition scheme of things—where trust is low, self-protective behavior is rampant, and so many people feel vulnerable—the egos belonging to high-talent personnel often get a little shaky.

Bruised egos cause many of the bailouts. Sometimes the people in question feel threatened. In other cases, people with a high need for attention and approval leave because they are being romanced by recruiters and more or less ignored by their own superiors. While it overstates the case, a guideline to go by is that high performers have developed a larger-than-average appetite for ego gratification. So a person's ego serves as a promising avenue for rerecruitment.

This argues for getting close to your good people, for making them feel special. The more they feel valued and important to the corporate cause, the better the chances that their job commitment will remain high and they will think in terms of staying with the organization.

Sometimes a big ego boost comes from giving this sort of person a key role, maybe an important assignment in the merger-integration process itself. And typically the ego gets pumped up if a person gets a better title or new perks that normally go with high rank or reputation.

Status symbols may come in the form of administrative assistants, larger offices, first-class travel, or bigger budgets. At management and employee levels, the symbols are perhaps smaller in scope or importance, but they are just as powerful in terms of how they feed people's work egos. Awards banquets, getting one's name printed in the company newspaper as a high achiever, and trips for reaching major goals all provide an ego boost.

But consider what happens so commonly in a merger. Imagine a $200 million company where executives, managers, and employees are operating a successful, profitable, growing business. Depending on their level in the organization, they can make decisions, allocate capital, respond to customers, set policy, and count on being paid for performance. Then, without much warning, their company is acquired. Soon they find themselves operating as a small, fairly insignificant division of a $12 billion conglomerate. Egos take a hit all across the organization, from top to bottom, and it is a hard thing for people to swallow. They now must abide by new rules and policies set by someone else. Their pay for performance gets replaced with a standard scale set by the acquiring company. Their budgets are cut. They see their latitude to make decisions and respond to customers impeded by a new level of oversight on the part of the acquirer. And the bigger the ego, the harder the hit.

Quick repair of key people's egos helps greatly in the rerecruitment of the organization's most important human capital. Simple actions—timely taken—counter the feelings of loosing status that often are associated with change. For example, key individuals might be flown to corporate headquarters to meet with parent company management. They might be given a little better office accommodations or better equipment to work with. Something as simple as a special dinner with senior management in the acquiring organization or one-on-one meetings to discuss their career opportunities in the new organization could be just the thing to salve the ego of someone on the verge of seeking a career opportunity elsewhere.

Doing the Right Thing   Whether it is in service of their career, family, or employees, people generally want to do what's right. The difficulty arises, however, when what seems right for one party is potentially not right for another. When organizations are involved in a merger/acquisition event, key personnel are ordinarily introduced to a new set of stakeholders: investors, analysts, new customers, employees, and others outside the company. During those times of change, the question is not only, "Are we doing the right things?" but also, "Who are we doing the right things *for?*" Resolving these questions is of paramount importance in making a merger successful. This is especially true in terms of how key people feel about the decisions being made in the change process. The answers heavily influence whether or not people will choose to commit themselves to helping with the integration effort.

It helps, as discussed earlier, to provide people with some sense of control. That gives them more of a feeling that the changes are the right thing to do because they personally have some say in them. But most of the time it is not practical, or perhaps even possible, to involve all of the key people in the decisions being made. In those situations where key people are unable to play an active part, the reasoning behind the decisions needs to be made clear. If people have a good sense of the rationale for change, they are better equipped to deal with the second question posed above, "Who are we doing the right things *for?*"

Obviously, some of the merger-related decisions are not based directly on what is right for specific personnel in the company but what is right for customers, shareholders, or overall company profitability. Still, doing what is right for the customers or the shareholder or profitability in general should have a positive impact on company personnel—at least in the long term, global sense. This impact commonly comes in the form of higher sales, greater market share, or better margins. And that translates into better chances for pay raises and promotions. Giving people this rationale for the decisions that are made probably won't make everyone happy. The idea, though, is to help them understand that staying on board and committing to making the changes successful is the right thing to do.

TURN THE MOTIVATORS INTO RERECRUITMENT ACTIONS

Once people's primary motivators are understood, they should be turned into action steps that correspond with rerecruiting specific individuals and groups throughout the organization. This should be organized as a formal plan— written down on paper—and truly should be *actionable*.

A well-crafted rerecruitment program will include measurement of how effective the effort has been. Many organizations already measure turnover rates on an annual basis. But in times of change, when rerecruitment becomes extremely important, measuring overall turnover in this manner is not sufficient. Time frames for turnover measurements need to be shortened.

For instance, turnover can be measured on a monthly basis. Historical turnover also should be converted to the same time basis, so an accurate comparison can be made between historical and current retention statistics. The rate at which people are leaving also should be tracked in a way that allows trouble spots among specific groups to be spotted early. For instance, turnover measurements might be broken down by rank or hierarchy, geographical location, work group or functional area, and so on.

In addition to tracking turnover, exit interviews should be performed with anyone who announces his or her departure. Because the merger environment accelerates the time frame in which information needs to be gathered, it is probably wise to conduct these exit interviews before the person's actual last working day. Regardless of when they are conducted, though, exit interviews can be a valuable tool for gaining insights that strengthen subsequent rerecruitment efforts.

It takes time to develop and execute a compelling rerecruitment strategy, and there are many competing demands for people's time. Far too often, there is virtually nothing done by way of deliberate rerecruitment, except for scattered attempts to hang on to a handful of upper-level executives. Usually, the measures taken to retain key talent are superficial, poorly coordinated, and carried out with a serious lack of urgency. This helps explain why so many merger/acquisition situations are marked by a mass exodus of valuable talent and why so many mergers end up in the failure statistics.

PART THREE

Meeting the Management Challenge

CHAPTER 8

Integration Project Management

Acquiring and merging involve more than just integration management. The coming together of two companies should be handled as a single, coordinated process. Too many companies make the mistake of separating the major phases of a deal (for example, due diligence, agreement, integration), when in fact these phases are always interconnected. Figure 8-1 shows the basic phases associated with any merger or acquisition.

The particular timing of these phases will vary from situation to situation, but relative timing is not the point here. The point is that integration cannot be divorced from any of the other phases and should not be treated as though it can be. Even in due diligence, there are important analyses and decisions being made that have an impact on integration.

The success of a deal is usually predicated on being able to carry out certain integration actions. Whether it is the consolidation of facilities in a particular region, the transfer of technologies needed to get a new product to market, or the enhancement of margins through increased purchasing power, these objectives need to be well documented from the outset. This helps create a common thread throughout all of

FIGURE 8-1

Integration Planning and Phases of a Merger

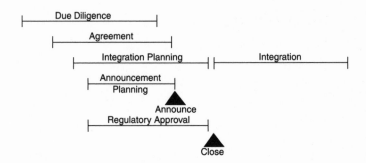

the major phases, and that is an important step in preparing for the many management challenges sure to come.

In order to maintain continuity from the courtship through the union of the organizations involved, the various phases should be dealt with under a single management umbrella. Putting a management structure in place early, and adding resources to it as activity increases, allows merging entities to get the head start they need in planning an integration and meeting the challenges head-on.

ASSESSING THE CHALLENGE

Managing the marriage of two companies is certainly one of the most difficult assignments one can face in the corporate world. Anyone who has led the implementation of a large information system or the relocation of a facility knows how many headaches can be associated with those sorts of challenges. But leading an integration involves all the problems of those projects plus an even longer list of management demands. In addition, all of these challenges must be handled in an environment characterized by complicated, high-pressure conditions. Table 8-1 details some

TABLE 8-1

Management Challenges and Complicating
Environmental Factors

Management Challenges	Complicated By
• Meeting aggressive deadlines	• Sagging morale
• Achieving tough financial targets	• Low trust level
	• Productivity drop-off
• Restructuring quickly with limited information	• Widespread uncertainty
• Merging a variety of systems applications and architectures	• Heightened competition
	• Culture clashes
• Retaining key employees	• Rumors
• Maintaining adequate communication	• Politics and positioning
	• Intense media scrutiny
• Managing relocations and consolidations	

of the difficulties that management must face during an integration and describes the unique circumstances that make it an unusually tough exercise. (These environmental factors are largely a result of the shock waves and problems described in Chapter 3.)

Because the convergence of these challenges occurs in a different environment than normally exists for managers, different approaches are required. Managing a merger, regardless of size, is distinctly different from managing an ongoing operation.

The first step one can take toward being an effective manager of mergers and acquisitions is to understand what a unique event they represent in the life cycle of an organization. As a method of corporate growth, they are revolutionary rather than evolutionary. And it is important to recognize that uncommon growth calls for uncommon solutions. This often means managing the transition in a fashion that seems counterintuitive or completely different from established organizational norms.

ORGANIZING FOR INTEGRATION

Mergers and acquisitions heat up the management atmosphere. There is so much to do at once and so much at stake. It is crucial to proceed with a clear sense of priorities, and this calls for a carefully structured approach.

Good integration management is characterized by discipline, focus, and dedicated resources. A project group should be formed to manage the transition, and it should operate as a parallel organization focusing purely on the integration process. This organization needs to be adequately staffed, with people's roles and responsibilities clearly defined. Several individuals should plan to devote their time fully to the project during the transition so that the integration process has the necessary direction and continuity.

Disorganization gets dangerous during transition. Let's face it, merging is confusing enough even when good project management practices are in place. Without that kind of discipline, the situation can all too easily spin out of control. This is a highly charged political climate where people operate with very different, personalized agendas. There are so many pressure points, conflicting points of view, and management distractions. Unless you employ a carefully orchestrated project management approach, it is almost impossible to get through the integration without damaging the potential of the deal.

Treating the transition period like a special project helps management achieve adherence to schedule, effective use of resources, a focus on true priorities, and responsible management of risk. That certainly makes it worth the effort. But beyond all that, taking a project management approach actually makes it much easier to get through the demanding integration process successfully. It helps prevent the haphazard, floundering efforts so often seen where a lack of good organization results in wasted motion, false starts, and divergent initiatives that emotionally drain the people involved, while producing very poor outcomes.

PROJECTS VERSUS OPERATIONS

Implementing a project management approach doesn't come naturally to some people. After all, most organizations are built around ongoing operations. And the skill set or techniques required to run a project are quite different from those that might make someone a star as an operating professional. Table 8-2 highlights some of the key differences between projects and operations.

What happens when there is an absence of the discipline and structure that a project management approach makes possible? Typically, the result is a poorly run integration that results in a resource drain, loss of focus for both organizations, and serious slippage in productivity.

A Fortune 50 company experienced this firsthand when it acquired a small semiconductor manufacturer with a reputation for strong design skills but weak manufacturing. The

TABLE 8-2

Contrasting Aspects of Operations and Projects

	Projects	Operations
Time frame	Clear start and end date	Ongoing
Resources	Constant change	Optimized/predictable
Risk management	Consolidate risk	Diversify risk
Reporting	One time	Repetitive
Success management	Based on final results	Based on constant review

organizational fit seemed to be obvious since the acquirer had a strong manufacturing capability and had identified semiconductor growth as a strategic objective. The acquisition appeared to be a win-win situation from the start. But because management felt the benefits would be easy to achieve, there was no formal integration risk assessment and no project plan created for managing the integration. Months later, it was still unclear how the integration would actually occur. A frustrated engineer in the parent company was heard to complain about the engineers in the acquired firm: "They act as if they acquired us!" Essentially, the two companies continued to operate as separate entities, and the potential benefits of the integration were never fully achieved.

"DOLLARIZING" THE COST OF A POORLY MANAGED INTEGRATION

You develop a higher respect for the value of using a project management approach by putting a dollar value on the cost of lost productivity. Research shows that a company can reasonably expect a 25 to 50 percent drop in productivity when going through large-scale change. The reasons for this are detailed in Chapter 3. Basically, people become preoccupied with the "me" issues, the organization's attention is focused inwardly, and all this results in a loss of corporate momentum and operating effectiveness.

It's easy to design a simple example that highlights the financial implications of this productivity downturn. Let's say "Roberts, Inc." is a small manufacturing company that has 262 employees with an average hourly labor cost, including benefits, of $32. If we assume a drop in productivity of only 1.5 hours each workday (a conservative estimate), the daily cost that can be attributed to the merger will be $262 \times 32 \times 1.5 = \$12,576$. If the integration is poorly managed, and thus takes two months longer than would be necessary with good project management, the total climbs up to $528,192 (assuming 20 business days per month).

If the organization is operating at an 8 percent profit margin, the sales force will need to generate an additional $4,225,536 in revenue to offset the drop in productivity. But keep in mind that it's far more likely that revenues will be sagging rather than hitting new highs.

PROJECT STRUCTURE AND ROLES

An efficient and serviceable structure for the project group consists of three different layers: a steering committee, a merger team, and a variety of task-force teams. Assuming that the appropriate people (in terms of personality, management ability, technical talent, and time to devote to the process) are assigned to these slots, the group is in a position to do a good job of integration management.

Typically, the steering committee is small, consisting of two to four individuals, all of whom are senior-level people. The focus of this group is to provide direction to the integration effort as it relates to strategy and policy. While not committed full-time to the process, this group should meet on a regularly scheduled basis to approve integration plans and review progress.

If it is a true merger situation, the group may benefit from equally balanced representation from the two organizations. If it's better defined as an acquisition situation, the steering committee may have a majority, or even all of its members, coming from the acquirer. But representation from both organizations helps ensure that key financial, operational, or cultural aspects are not overlooked during the integration process.

Executive sponsorship is critical to the success of the integration. As the integration moves forward, there will be resistance from both individuals and departments. This opposition may result from a conflict with some operating priority ("You're interfering with our annual planning cycle.") or protection of the status quo ("It's always been done this way, and we don't need to change it now."). Senior-level personnel who serve on the steering committee may be the only ones with the necessary clout to get past these obstacles. The steering committee will also need to act as the final decision point for resource allocation and prioritizing of the recommended initiatives.

The merger team, consisting of some three to five full-time people, is the real workhorse responsible for driving the integration forward and keeping good project management discipline in place. One member of this team should be designated as the integration project leader and given the overall responsibility for the project's progress. As a whole, this team's purpose is to provide the guidance and day-to-day decision making that will allow the integration process to move forward on a timely basis. This group also should include members of both organizations. A fairly balanced representation generally fosters better buy-in from the people in the two organizations while also improving the odds that plans for integration can be implemented effectively.

The third level of the project management structure is comprised of a number of task-force teams. These units ordinarily are comprised of three to five people and are formed to address specific organizational issues needing attention because of the merger/acquisition event. They can be either resource driven, such as finance, human resources, information technology, and so on, or operations driven according to business unit, product line, or perhaps geographic location. The resource-driven teams will have tasks of their own to complete but also will need to support the operating groups in the completion of their respective tasks. The task-force teams commonly have individuals working both full-time and part-time on the integration and should have one person designated as the team leader.

The assortment of task-force teams take their marching orders from, and report to, the merger team. In turn, the merger team is ultimately accountable to the steering committee. Under the day-to-day direction of the integration project leader, the merger team has responsibility for coordinating all of the analyses and recommendations for action that the task-force teams generate.

PROJECT LIFE CYCLE

It is helpful to look at the integration process as a logical sequence of steps designed to help bring the two organizations together. Breaking the integration process into five discrete phases—envision, assess, deploy, manage, and close—makes it easier to get mentally organized for the overall task at hand.

Envision

This initial stage is all about laying the groundwork for successful integration. The steering committee focuses on building the project structure to link the objectives of the integration with the strategic intent of the merger. A formal project structure is defined, and an overall project leader is assigned. People are tapped to serve on the merger team, and that group is given the charter that will guide its activities throughout the project. Task-force teams also are identified, and appropriate operating charters are developed for each team. The steering committee and merger team work together to create an integration strategy that identifies critical content areas where task-force teams will focus their efforts. The overall schedule for the integration project should be established, too, along with the various timelines denoting when certain integration activities should take place.

Assess

The merger team carries responsibility for managing the process of evaluating current operations and recommending changes based on integration requirements. So this stage is characterized by diagnostics and analysis. Granted, the due diligence effort generated some degree of data about how the integration process might be carried out. But this is an opportunity for a more in-depth, close-range examination.

If it wasn't done in the *envision* stage, now is the time to establish the success measures that will be used to gauge the effectiveness of the integration process. Essentially, this means establishing the goalposts for the project. This exercise enables the integration effort to proceed in a much more purposeful fashion. It's the kind of drill that helps bring coherence and coordinated effort to the integration process.

One of the tasks to be completed in this phase is the comparison of original budgets with the current environment. The financials of the deal need to be reviewed by task-force teams as they assess the extent of integration that should occur. This leads to better prioritization of key activities and the most appropriate allocation of resources.

This is also the time to revisit the risk assessments done during the due diligence phase. Teams identify new risks that may need to be added and then help craft contingency plans and mitigation strategies to control those risks. Both immediate and long-term resource requirements also should be determined. Some skills or resources may not be available and will either need to be acquired or sourced before parts of the integration plan may proceed.

Deploy

As the various task-force teams get their assignments under way, a more accurate understanding of needs and objectives will evolve. As German Field Marshall von Clausewitz said,

"No plan survives contact with the enemy." The same can be said about project management. As soon as you begin to deploy resources around a task, new information surfaces that allows the people involved to gain a better assessment of the costs, opportunities, upcoming problems, and most appropriate time frames for the integration. Managing a merger is an organic process. Regardless of how detailed the program for integration might be, a generous amount of improvising is still required.

A key assignment for the task-force teams will be capturing all associated costs of the integration and determining how they should be classified. Specifically, should they be handled as one-time integration costs or as costs associated with ongoing operations? It is critical that the financial implications of the merger or acquisition be accounted for properly so that an appropriate assessment of future performance can be made.

Manage

As the integration process proceeds, the merger team must work with the task-force teams to monitor the integration against schedule and budget. This allows the merger team to adjust resources as necessary and, of course, enables it to keep the steering committee informed of progress in merging the two organizations. Status reporting is an important discipline. Tight control should be exercised to ensure that the various task-force leaders submit their updates on time, according to a preestablished format, and with a thorough account of the teams' work to date.

Close

The final phase of the integration process involves the handoff from the merger integration project group to the appropriate operating groups. At this time, it's also important to assess the quality of the transition effort to determine what changes might be appropriate during the next integration. If a firm plans additional mergers and acquisitions as an active business strategy, it should conduct a formal debriefing at the end of the integration process as a way of further developing its competencies in the merger-integration process.

COMMON MISTAKES IN INTEGRATION PROJECT MANAGEMENT

As a quick wrap-up on the subject, six frequent errors in the way organizations handle the integration process will be highlighted. These are seen all too often even in well-run companies with highly capable executives at the helm.

1. Lack of a clearly defined project leader. Make sure one person is put in charge of the integration effort. Assigning individual accountability and responsibility is the best way to get a strong action orientation in support of the integration project. Some organizations choose one person from each organization to serve as coleaders in the process. While this may seem equitable, it can lead to confusion as to who has formal sign-off over a given task or activity, or who is ultimately responsible for the success or failure of the transition effort. Generally it's a good idea to make sure that individuals from both organizations are present on the team, but it works best when only one person is in charge.

2. Failure to execute against plan. Transition teams often find it is easier to develop a plan than it is to execute one. The program for action should not be so complicated that it cannot be carried out. The role of the merger team is to ensure that the plan is manageable and that the task-force teams do not become sidetracked.

3. Declaring victory on the 20-yard line. Avoid the temptation to proclaim that the merger is over just because some important, top-level issues have been settled. The chairman of a large managed care company came before his people, stating that the integration was complete once the senior management team had been identified. He felt that each executive would handle integration concerns within his or her respective operating areas. For lack of a coordinated ongoing effort, the integration proceeded at different speeds in different parts of the organization. The result was a clumsy, poorly executed integration.

4. Skimping on the investment in the integration effort. Companies often invest heavily in due diligence, then get remarkably stingy in terms of their willingness to spend on the integration effort. This helps explain why so many good deals go bad. A strategy for growth through mergers is carefully conceived but poorly implemented. The economics argue strongly in favor of allocating sufficient resources— money and people—to support a sophisticated integration process.

5. Presuming that all people are at the same point. Senior management typically spends months planning a merger or acquisition. Invariably, they are way ahead of the rest of the people in terms of having adjusted to the situation. They've had access to information, time to wrestle with the issues, and—likely as not—already have closure on how they personally will be affected by the deal. Other folks will be lagging far behind. Remember this when communicating to the rest of the organization. Design an aggressive communication plan to get people the information they need. Move at top speed to give them closure on the "me issues."

6. Leaving too much on the table. Too many integration efforts are far too superficial. Often, companies are satisfied if they can merely get the benefits outlined in the initial deal announcement. But usually more juice can be squeezed out of the merger. For example, is there a technology in one of the companies that can be used in the product line of the other company? Has each task-force team taken a good, hard look at the combined organization to find every possible benefit? Seek out every possible synergy? Continue to look for cost cutting and revenue growth beyond what the deal makers originally identified?

CHAPTER 9

Fundamentals of Successful Strategy

Good integration management can salvage a poorly crafted deal. And it can turn a well-conceived merger into a blazing success. Invariably, management is unable to prevent or solve as many problems as they would wish, regardless of how carefully they orchestrate the integration strategy. But by adhering to a set of fundamentals, the people in charge can ensure that the problems so generic to mergers are not allowed to destroy the potential value of the deal.

The point has already been made that a project management approach should be applied to the integration process. A project infrastructure should be established that will support flexibility and speed while also bringing discipline to the effort. Now for a fuller explanation of the argument for moving through the integration with a strong sense of urgency.

POSTMERGER DRIFT

Corporate marriages are rarely followed by honeymoons. Employees in the acquired organization, as well as those executives responsible for striking the deal, tell endless war stories of the problems, frustrations, and surprises that commonly follow on the heels of a merger. Once the marriage has been consummated, there is little time for celebration. If there is a honeymoon, it is short-lived. In the best of circumstances, it is followed by a "little period of adjustment." Of course, a big percentage of the time, there is severe marital trauma, which lasts much longer than necessary.

The problems companies have in managing the change process are manifested in many ways during the months, and even years, that follow the merger event. Almost always there is a lull, a loss of momentum in the acquired firm.

Experience shows that in most mergers the greatest lull happens during the first few months. Companies then slowly revitalize, taking a period of one or two years to fully recover. Some, of course, never seem the same, although the initial intent was for the acquisition to represent some sort of synergistic hookup between the two organizations.

This phenomenon is comparable to the postoperative period of recuperation experienced by the patient who undergoes surgery. That person usually shows a drop-off in productivity. His or her morale usually suffers until physical and emotional strength are regained. And she or he will have difficulty mobilizing personal resources in order to perform effectively.

Acquired companies usually struggle through a similar adjustment process. The severity of the episode depends heavily on the nature of the takeover—whether it was fiercely resisted or jointly sought. But the results are almost always counterproductive so far as productivity, profitability, employee motivation, and morale are concerned. In fact, postmerger drift has become such a common occurrence that it is basically viewed as an inherent reality within the merger process, as something that just goes with the territory.

The intensity and persistence of postmerger drift can be controlled and kept to a minimum. But to overcome this interlude, the parent company will nearly always need to

take a hands-on approach. Top executives must move decisively and purposefully—not simply to make changes, but
to make the right changes and then intelligently manage the
organizational dissonance a merger creates.

If people are allowed to respond to their natural in-
stincts, many of them will move into a holding pattern.
Depending on the parent company's reaction, the downward
trend that develops usually bottoms out within a three- to
nine-month period. Then begins the gradual and often halt-
ing uptrend over the next year or so. Eventually, corporate
effectiveness should equal, and hopefully surpass, the premerger level. Sometimes, of course, it never does.

Figure 9-1 charts the common pattern of organizational
performance during the first two years following acquisition.
Operating effectiveness suffers from the psychological shock
waves and resulting reactions of employees. Just how much
deterioration there is in operating effectiveness, and how
long it lasts, is dependent on (1) what kind of acquisition
scenario is involved and (2) how astutely the company is
managed after the fact.

FIGURE 9-1

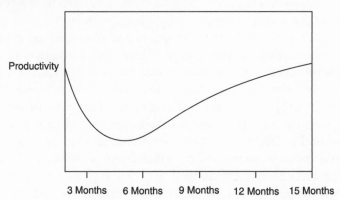

Postmerger Recovery Period

The situation calls for proactive, take-charge management. Problems always get a head start, and this means that managers and executives are always put in a position of having to play catch-up. Another argument for fast action comes from the fact that people being acquired and merged *expect* change. They become anxious and uncomfortable if the acquirer, having finalized the deal, pulls back and assumes a passive stance. Granted, incumbents don't want to be manhandled or overwhelmed with changes, but they don't want to be ignored either. The most common complaint from people involved in a merger has to do with the acquirers' lack of action or excessively slow pace.

TRUST IN SPEED

In years past, the conventional wisdom on the integration process advocated a slow transition. The rationale went like this: This is important. We must move slowly, carefully, and minimize mistakes. We can't afford to overwhelm people with change.

It all sounded so logical. It seemed like such a caring approach so far as the people were concerned. The problem is, the thinking was dead wrong.

Basically, employees hate a slow integration process. The approach lets problems fester, and it fails to take advantage of the energy stirred up by a merger event.

Being careful during mergers and acquisitions means moving quickly. Speed is your ally. A rapid integration approach that reflects a strong sense of urgency holds far more promise than a strategy based on caution. The mistakes that come from going fast are nothing compared to the problems of going too slow. Just imagine the impact of a 20 to 30 percent drop in the effectiveness of a sales organization when the integration process drags on for six months or so. What if the transition lasts 24 months instead of 6? What if the productivity drop is 50 percent instead of 30? Slow transitions have significant damaging impact to the bottom line.

At the very outset, it is important to set the expectation for moving quickly through the integration process. The parent company should convey an image of urgency, demonstrating that the new regime is action oriented. The "opening moves" should be designed to illustrate the pace the acquirer intends to maintain. Appropriate initial steps communicate that the new organizational framework will not be a do-nothing, life-as-usual setup.

It also should be emphasized here that the employees of the acquired company will draw their conclusions about the parent company by observing what it *does*, rather than from listening to what its senior executives *say*. In fact, there will be a great deal of skepticism regarding what the acquirer says or writes, whereas anything actually done represents hard data.

The question that should be posed, then, is "What is fast?" Some organizations might speed up noticeably yet still fall far short of showing the metabolism needed in the integration process.

London Life Insurance Company of London, Ontario (Canada), provides a good model. In 1996, London Life acquired the Canadian operations of The Prudential Insurance Company of America. The marriage of these two organizations was no simple task, with nearly $20 billion (CN$) in assets involved. But London Life and The Prudential of Canada went to work early and quickly. On a single day, six full weeks before the announcement was made, integration planning gained momentum. It started at 8 A.M. one Tuesday morning. By 10 A.M. the structure was defined. By 2 P.M. people were identified for each task team and notified about their assignment. At 6:30 P.M. a dinner was held for a collection of 30 senior managers and task-force members, many of whom were hearing about the acquisition for the first time. At dinner, the approach was presented and modified. The next day, task forces that had been formed met to begin planning for pre- and post-announcement integration. All of this speed on the front end led to an extremely successful announcement in which questions from employees, the media, analysts, customers, and suppliers could be answered in a definitive manner. This fast start allowed the integration to move forward much more quickly than originally thought possible. The success in this case was due largely to expectations for moving rapidly being established up front. In addition, senior management openly acknowledged that some mistakes undoubtedly would be made, and they asked for forgiveness at the very beginning of the transition.

REEVALUATE PRIORITIES

While speed and efficiency during an integration are important, effectiveness is just as critical. The announcement of an acquisition introduces new information to an organization. It changes the landscape. This requires a reevaluation of existing activities. Organizations will find that, upon announcement of an acquisition, many projects are no longer critical. Others need to be modified or should be delayed in light of new priorities.

One large electronics manufacturer that had just been acquired found that an implementation of SAP software could be halted due to capabilities already existing at the parent company. Reengineering efforts, new product launches, R&D efforts, and strategic planning processes can all be affected by a merger or acquisition. Reevaluating priorities early in the process helps prevent concurrent pressures from vying for people's time and energy, while ensuring that the most financially beneficial initiatives are pursued first.

ENGINEER EARLY WINS

Unfortunately, large transitions such as mergers are by nature riddled with problems. These difficulties are not necessarily indications of a poorly conceived merger, bad management, or a weak integration strategy. Instead, they are usually merely signs that a merger is happening.

Trying to convince people of this fact is tough. And trying to convince merger *critics* is nearly impossible. To make things worse, the critics get their "proof" that the merger is "bad" long before the supporters manage to get their evidence to the contrary. As pointed out in Chapter 3, mergers invariably produce a set of generic problems, and the antimerger crowd uses this to support its case. To battle this strong negative sentiment, it is important to engineer some early wins. In other words, management should quickly identify some easy ways to capture successes, make sure those successes are achieved, and then publicize them widely.

For instance, one large, international computer reseller was able to take advantage of a purchasing system in the company it had just acquired. The company quickly upgraded its software with help from the information systems group in the target company. As a result, it was able to solve several long-standing problems related to accuracy and efficiency in processing purchase orders. The actions were publicized in the company newsletter as evidence that the combination of the companies could be beneficial.

In another case, a large Fortune 50 manufacturing company quickly approved the investment of $100,000 for a new manufacturing line to be located at the acquired organization's site. This was an early win for both the acquirer (it normally took six weeks for capital approval) and for the acquiree (they sorely needed the excess capacity and enhanced capability).

KEEP YOUR EYE ON THE BALL

Major organizational change causes a company to become more introspective. This is especially true during merger integration. Once a deal is announced, the focus of both organizations turns inward. Because of this internal orientation, companies often get distracted from the actual running of the business.

The most vulnerable areas of the organization are sales, service, and information systems—that is, the key contact points with the customer and the infrastructure that supports them. Many organizations experience a drop in sales and increased complaints about customer service shortly after a merger. It's something merging organizations can ill afford to let happen. The company is already caught in the glare of the spotlight, with analysts, management, employees (of both organizations), and customers all studying how the deal will affect business. If sales and service start to suffer, people blame the merger and typically begin to question the viability of the decision to merge. Moreover, customers begin fleeing to competitors, complaining that service has now been abandoned by the merging organizations. Shareholders get spooked by noise from the analysts and dump their stock. Employees may jump ship because they fear for the company's future.

Management must see that these key areas are protected. Special attention is needed to protect sales and maintain service standards. The situation calls for new initiatives—high-powered programs that catch people's attention and produce results. This might include short-term sales incentives or merger training and information for customer service personnel at help desks and call centers. Another possibility might be special advertising aimed at communicating to customers the newly merged organization's commitment to service. Whatever the particular prescription, actions to boost sales and service must be deliberately planned and quickly executed.

EXPLOIT THE INSTABILITY

It is important not only to survive during the instability created by the merger or acquisition but to thrive on it, to exploit the upheaval. Managers commonly react by attempting to stabilize the organization during the transition, seeking to return things to normal. But this is an impossible task as well as a wasted opportunity. Instead of spending energy on a fruitless pursuit of normalcy, management should use the transition period as an opportunity to make needed changes that may be entirely unrelated to the merger. People are expecting change. The company is in a state of flux anyway. And you can accomplish things that would be far more difficult, if not impossible, under routine circumstances.

In particular, changes that are widely recognized as sorely needed and long overdue can be made concurrent with the integration. Of course, the importance of proposed changes must be weighed against integration initiatives. More often than not, a few changes will have long been recognized as having tremendous financial implications and strategic value. Now is the time to capitalize on the instability and get these changes implemented.

COMMUNICATE HIGH EXPECTATIONS

Executives should challenge the workforce of the acquired company by setting fresh and somewhat higher standards of performance. This is a highly appropriate time to make people stretch.

As already mentioned, mergers and acquisitions cause people to examine their behavior and reevaluate their modus operandi. This introspection, plus the destabilizing effect of the merger/acquisition, causes them to be much more open to behavior change. Astute executives will seize this opportunity to call more of the employees' potential into play.

It is important, however, that any new and more demanding standards of performance be communicated clearly. And parent company executives should express confidence in people's ability to measure up. It is not enough to just notch up the bars so that the hurdles are higher. Employees must grasp the idea that the parent company believes in them and their ability to make the grade.

Most people upgrade their performance automatically when confronted with a leader who expects more of them and expresses confidence in their ability to measure up. What so frequently happens in the postmerger setting, though, is (1) expectations are not communicated clearly at all, and (2) employees in the acquired firm somehow get the idea that the parent company views them as less capable or as possessing questionable ability to meet new performance standards. As a result, people in the acquired firm become less motivated and suffer a loss of confidence.

Generally speaking, employees would prefer to contend with higher performance requirements that are made clear rather than blurred, ill-defined standards that aren't particularly demanding. They just want to know how the measuring stick works and who will do the measuring. Finally, they respond favorably to high expectations when it seems that top management genuinely has faith in their ability to achieve them.

PROVIDE A SENSE OF CORPORATE DIRECTION

Just as people can be challenged to perform better when they are confronted with more demanding expectations, they also are motivated to upgrade performance when they are given a clear sense of direction. The acquirer who steps forth promptly to structure organizational goals for employees provides a crucial focus for organizational resources. Many of the conventional problems associated with mergers and acquisitions are a direct offshoot of people going off on tangents, operating in a fog, or essentially shifting into neutral for lack of well-defined goals.

Research has proved convincingly that resources, whether individual or organizational, will gravitate toward clear goals. But employees in an acquired firm routinely are left to operate for months without any clearly defined targets.

Parent company executives may intend for the acquisition to continue running on the same set of tracks in pursuit of the same corporate objectives. But incumbents frequently are not convinced that this is really the case, even if the new owner says so. Employees are inclined to remain skeptical until it is obvious that the acquirer understands the existing goals and reaffirms them in writing.

Of course, all too often, the acquired firm (or at least part of it) has been operating without a set of specific, concrete, and measurable goals that are well integrated. Various departments or corporate functions may be working at cross-purposes. Some parts of the company may be wandering aimlessly. Still others may be charging ahead with a vengeance but actually going in the wrong direction. These situations seriously undermine organizational effectiveness and certainly indicate a need for the acquirer to intervene.

Newly merged or acquired organizations need road maps with well-charted routes and specific destinations. But it is very common for employees to muddle around for a year or more before they finally figure out what is going on and where the new company is headed. Top management needs to move with great haste to get people focused on the future rather than allowing them to wallow in uncertainty or the nostalgia of "the way we were."

At this stage of the game, people benefit from an intense focus on short-term targets. Long-term goal setting requires more time and effort and involves more guesswork. Furthermore, people will benefit from seeing short-range goals achieved. It pumps them up, builds confidence, and restores momentum to the corporate machine. Some of the interim goals or short-term objectives should be related to the merger situation itself. That is, they should be transition goals designed to help facilitate the integration process.

In the process of framing these new goals and operating objectives, management should take great pains to see that the goals are well synchronized. It is easy for different people to come forth promoting conflicting objectives, such that individuals or groups end up working at odds. There is little value in having managers push hard for the attainment of their respective priorities when they end up in hot pursuit of incompatible objectives.

Of course, it's not enough just to set goals, or even to make sure that those goals are well synchronized. They have to be communicated to the people who will be responsible for their achievement. This calls for a lot of publicity. Management needs to keep the spotlight on the targets that have been established. It is also important to provide regular, frequent, and specific feedback regarding progress toward goal achievement.

Employee performance is greatly enhanced when people are given sharply defined goals together with frequent readings regarding their performance. In the postmerger environment, these elements so often are missing. The result is that people get mired down and preoccupied with the here and now instead of attacking the future in a vigorous, well-focused manner.

TAKE AN AFFIRMING STANCE

For most people in an acquired firm, the acquisition is a threatening experience. It creates feelings of uncertainty. In fact, when top management is simply taking some of the steps recommended here—for example, communicating more demanding expectations or establishing a new corporate direction—employees grow more uneasy. The natural tendency is to become more inhibited in work behavior. People move more cautiously and are less willing to take reasonable risks that would actually benefit the organization.

Parent company personnel frequently foster inhibitions and fuel employee concerns unintentionally. This happens when their attitude toward people in the acquired firm is impatient, critical, or condescending. Mergers make people at all levels more hypersensitive, and their pride is easily injured. It takes very little provocation to put them on the defensive or demotivate them.

Parent company executives should take pains to establish and maintain a congenial climate—that is, one that is encouraging, supportive, and positive. All of the people in the parent firm who will have direct contact with acquisition employees should be given formal coaching on how to best enter the acquisition and how to interface with people there. Personnel from the parent firm should be instructed to take advantage of any opportunity to praise individuals and groups—publicly, privately, in writing, or in person. The new organizational climate should be affirming rather than critical, encouraging rather than threatening, challenging rather than inhibiting. Employees in the acquisition respond best when given a feeling of importance.

Many employees in the acquired firm will be frustrated with the feeling that they have to prove themselves anew to a cadre of unfamiliar executives. This frustration is further aggravated if the acquirer descends on the target firm like an invading army that has conquered and is sending in occupation troops. So it's a time for humility on the part of all representatives of the parent firm, as well as a time for ego-building efforts to be directed toward people in the acquisition.

GIVE PEOPLE A FLAG TO WAVE

If the new workforce is to be integrated, truly merged, then generally the sooner the better. People in the acquired firm need to be given a sense of citizenship in the new corporate structure. Demotivation rapidly sets in when top management in the parent firm chooses to straddle the fence, neither assimilating the workforce nor confirming that it will operate as an independent acquisition.

Companies suffer a loss of identity upon being acquired, and with that loss there usually is an erosion of commitment.

Motivation deteriorates as "the company" becomes a less well-defined entity to which people can maintain an emotional attachment. Furthermore, personal ties to upper-level managers or the owner may be severed as these people leave the scene, eliminating important personal loyalties that previously generated strong motivational forces.

Of course, there are some companies whose acquisitional philosophy has done little to threaten corporate identity. They make a deliberate effort to let acquisitions keep their individuality. Each subsidiary continues to use its own name and company colors.

If the acquisition's old corporate identity is to be eliminated, however, the parent (or surviving) firm has an obligation to bring acquisition employees into the fold. They need to be given a sense of the parent company's history and indoctrinated with its values, norms, and corporate philosophy. Naturally, this should be done in such a way that does not offend. It should not be delivered as propaganda or look like an attempt to brainwash but should represent an honest and businesslike effort to communicate the new corporate culture and the role the newcomers will play.

NAIL DOWN ROLES, RESPONSIBILITIES, AND WORKING RELATIONSHIPS

Immediately after the deal has been consummated, all echelons of management in the acquired company need a redefinition of their authority, reporting relationships, and accountability. Additionally, they should be given a crystal-clear understanding of the standards of performance they will be expected to achieve.

These steps should be taken as quickly as possible after the consummation of the deal. If necessary, the acquirer should sacrifice detail for speed. The main thing is not to leave acquisition employees operating in a vacuum, or some will do nothing while others do wrong. Either way, they usually create secondary problems that then must be addressed. These are the causes of so many postmerger brush fires that distract top management from maintaining a major focus on corporate integration.

It is commonplace for an acquirer to assume that it has done a satisfactory job of communicating to people who's in charge, who reports to whom, and what's expected of everyone. But people constantly complain about confusing lines of authority and an ill-defined power structure. Employees feel they are operating in too much of a fog. The situation breeds frustration and tangled relationships, with the result being still another blow to employee motivation. Acquirers should recognize that, until these issues have been sorted out, people cannot complete the adjustment process and become fully reconciled to the merger/acquisition.

CHAPTER 10

General Guidelines for Merger/Acquisition Management

"This is a much harder job than I thought it would be." So said Robert Frankenberg, CEO of Novell, Inc., on the merger of Novell and WordPerfect. (*The Wall Street Journal*, January 12, 1996, p.1.)

Almost always, a large percentage of the people in charge are unprepared for the high-pressure demands of managing mergers and acquisitions. The following recommendations are offered as a quick wrap-up, with the hope that they will enable managers and executives to take a number of preventive steps to make the job easier.

COACHING POINTS FOR MANAGERS AND EXECUTIVES IN THE ACQUIRING FIRM

1. Don't promise that things will remain the same in either company. Most people won't believe you anyway, and most of those who do will later insist that you have lied or misrepresented things to them. Explain that there will be changes, but that extreme effort will be made to (a) consider the interests of each employee and (b) keep

143

them as well informed as possible of forthcoming changes. Remember, if you acquire another organization and don't make some changes, the odds are 10 to 1 that you have failed to take advantage of outstanding opportunities to make various changes that would be constructive, that are needed, and that incumbents would adapt to quite well.

It is risky to be emphatic in proclaiming, "We plan no management changes," even when that is the truth. Likely as not, some employees will put you in the position of having to terminate them, and you will be accused of reneging on your promise.

2. Make few promises. In addition to the admonitions offered in the preceding guideline, you should realize that promises of any type, as a general rule, will end up making life harder for you. In fact, even when you communicate something through innuendo, you can create expectations that will later prove to be a problem. Your hints will often be taken as hard data.

3. Keep your promises. When you do go on record as making a commitment, be as good as your word. There is a tremendous need in the postmerger environment for you to instill confidence and concentrate on developing a high degree of credibility. Do everything you can to raise the trust level. Understand that target company employees' paranoia, guardedness, and suspicion are very natural reactions to the situation.

4. Talk in specifics whenever you can. Try not to add to the ambiguity. Try to be structured in your approach. What seems obvious to you is often unfamiliar and complex to others. Explain things in clear, straightforward language—avoid in-house jargon—and don't be too sketchy or talk in too-general terms. Always check for understanding.

5. Be acutely aware of the impact of your comments, even in routine conversation. People will be trying to read things into almost everything you say. You are under a microscope now. An offhand remark or slip of the tongue, and one of the best people in the target company could be gone. Discretion is critical.

6. Don't feed the rumor mill. Again, a casual remark or careless wording can crank up another rumor when you should be doing everything you can to short-circuit rumors, conjecture, and misinformation.

7. Provide more communication than usual during and after the merger/acquisition event. Strive to overcome the information vacuum that typically develops. Maintain closer-than-usual contact because everyone becomes increasingly hungry for information.

Mergers and acquisitions cause the communication channels to grow longer, as more people are involved and the distance from decision centers increases. Furthermore, information often begins to travel along different paths, and this makes it easy for some people to get left out of the loop inadvertently.

8. If you don't have the answer people in the acquired firm need, help them find it. Don't be responsible for giving them the runaround. Instead of being a buck passer, fill the role of problem solver.

9. In keeping with the preceding guideline, you should strive to go the extra mile. Be helpful. Look for opportunities to facilitate the merger process. Anticipate the needs, and the questions, of people in the other organization. Then take the initiative in meeting those needs. Get the idea across that you are on their side. This can help defuse adversarial relations.

10. Listen with the third ear. Pay attention to *how* something is said, as well as to the actual verbal content of the message. The *way* someone in the acquired firm communicates may provide you with better information than do the words themselves. Be alert to implied meanings and hidden agendas. Deal with the total message: what's not said as well as what is, what's implied as well as what's said, the nonverbal as well as the verbal.

11. Be humble. Go out of your way to avoid behaving in a manner that might be construed as arrogant, superior, critical, abrasive, and the like. People in the acquired firm will be defensive. Don't threaten or intimidate, even accidentally, as there is enough anxiety out there already. Be respectful.

12. Overall, exercise your best public relations skills. Make people in the acquired firm feel important. Help make them feel they are a welcome part of the corporate family, not a stepchild or second-class citizen. Show empathy and patience. Be personal and try to have a human touch.

13. Be prompt. Act expeditiously. Even if you make a concerted effort to be timely, the acquired firm is almost certain to feel that things are proceeding too sluggishly, that it is taking too long to make decisions and take action.

Mergers and acquisitions mean that, in conducting business, things have to go through more channels. Decision making will be more blurred. Procedures will be changing and therefore more confusing. Do everything conceivable to tighten the response time.

14. Provide a clear sense of direction. Be purposeful. Any acquisition is more likely to be responsive to new leadership if there is straightforward communication regarding what the new leaders want done and how the acquired organization is expected to work toward those goals.

Respect the fact that uncertainty at the top increases the resistance to change at the lower levels. The acquired workforce and management team are far more likely to rally and do battle for a new administration's goals if that leadership sounds the charge in an unambiguous fashion.

15. Keep people in the acquired firm focused and future-oriented. Make the targets specific, measurable, realistic, and yet challenging. Set definite timetables and deadlines. In the absence of goals that can provide a good sense of direction, the workforce often shifts into neutral and begins to drift or coast.

16. Do one of two things: embrace the people and make them yours, or terminate them and get them out as quickly as possible. Get the surgery done with, then get on with business. Don't cut here, slice there, and after a while saw another limb off. Let the bleeding be done with so the healing can commence.

17. Don't just assume the acquired company will follow the parent company's rules, policies, and procedures without being told what they are. In fact, employees of the acquired company probably will have to be told a number of times before the message takes hold as it should.

18. Guard against a common mistake in underestimating the time and planning required to appropriately manage the change process associated with mergers and acquisitions. Experience shows that small acquisitions often call for just as much attention and sometimes more handholding and getting-adjusted time than the large ones.

19. Establish clear, well-defined reporting relationships and lines of authority. Historically, the most unsuccessful mergers and acquisitions have suffered from unclear relationships and a tendency to change already vague, poorly defined reporting relationships several times in the first year.

20. Coach the parent company managers you plan to "send across" into the acquisition regarding how you want them to make their entrance or debut. This deserves a day of careful training involving discussion of the situation, consideration of cultural differences, plus an analysis of personalities and the management style people are accustomed to in the acquired firm.

21. Resist any inclination to fight back at employees in the acquired firm. *Expect* resentment, hostility, and criticism. Absorb it and talk beyond it when you deal with these people.

22. Don't relax once the merger/acquisition legalities have been consummated. Now comes the critical period of making the deal work.

23. Make a concerted effort to minimize corporate staff interference, especially by middle-management personnel from the parent organization. Don't blitz the acquired firm with people who go in unannounced or unexplained.

24. Demonstrate a high regard for the limits of all available resources when establishing goals and timetables for the acquired firm. Objectives should be challenging but not unrealistic. You should strive to engineer success experiences rather than structure goals that are likely to be an exercise in frustration and futility. It is critical for your first few actions vis-à-vis the acquisition to be positive and successfully carried out. These first steps set the tone for the relationship and have far-reaching ramifications.

25. Be wary of replacing successful methods and procedures in the acquisition with new corporate rules from the parent company.

26. Guard against overwhelming the acquired company with paperwork, new reporting requirements, and so on. Get people in the acquisition to help determine which existing reports and paperwork chores can be eliminated or perhaps allowed to remain in lieu of parent-company requirements.

27. Realize you can't keep everybody happy.

COACHING POINTS FOR MANAGERS AND EXECUTIVES IN THE ACQUIRED ORGANIZATION

There is, quite naturally, generous overlap between the actions that should be taken by this group and by the parent-company management team. Nevertheless, those items will be reiterated here in the form of instructions to incumbent managers in the acquisition.

1. Expect change. Prepare for it. Instead of fighting or resisting, embrace it. Posture yourself as a change agent or, at least, as a facilitator.

Don't let yourself be surprised by the changes you will see or that you are expected to implement. Look toward the future, rather than futilely grasping the past and the old way of doing things.

2. Anticipate. Demonstrate a new level of initiative and resourcefulness. Look for ways to contribute to the integration process. The organization and particularly your people need more from you now than they have in routine times.

3. Stay goal directed. See that you operate with a sense of purpose, rather than moving into a holding pattern. Operate with clear-cut, specific objectives, even if they have to be very short-range. Establish interim goals relative to the merger process itself.

4. Provide subordinates a generous amount of management direction. Don't let your part of the organization fall victim to postmerger drift for lack of leadership and direction.

Employees need job structure. Give them a thorough set of marching orders, including clear objectives with definite timetables.

5. Become a role model for a positive attitude toward the merger. Guard against being an insurgent, one who implicitly legitimizes a negative attitude toward the merger.

Look at it this way: If you didn't leave, you decided to stay. Subordinates will be very sensitive to your attitude, however subtle the signals you send out.

6. Put more into your communication efforts. Invite input from subordinates and listen better. Then read between the lines. Consider the need for more frequent meetings with subordinates to provide more opportunity for two-way communication.

7. Demonstrate maximum openness and candor (exercising prudence and the necessary discretion, of course). But don't feed the rumor mill with speculation, conjecture, or damaging hearsay.

8. Guard against making extremist statements or taking unnecessary stands vis-à-vis the merger.

9. Make few promises, even though people will be pressing you for hard-and-fast answers. Be wary of making commitments you may be unable to keep.

10. Be sensitive to shifts in the power structure. It is likely that the merger will result in changes in the way things get done or in the way decisions are made. Go with the flow. Make the appropriate adjustments.

11. Motivate to the hilt. Mergers destabilize and create dissonance in an organization. They serve as an unfreezing event, and this sort of organizational shake-up gets people's attention. It rattles their cages, making them introspect, evaluate their performance or worth, and consider the need for behavior change. The time is right to push for new and better behavior / performance. Capitalize on the motivating potential the merger creates. It is a tremendous opportunity to reenergize people and organizations that have grown complacent and perhaps a bit stale.

12. Expect slower response times. Usually procedures are in a state of flux. Policies are changing. More people, and new people, are involved in the decision-making process. Often there is a lack of clarity regarding just exactly who should be included in problem-solving and decision-making activities. Keep in mind that information flow has to cover greater distances and involve more people than before.

13. Make the acquisition a two-way street. Get to know the other firm better. Learn how they do business. Make an effort to understand the parent company's values and management philosophy. Get a clear fix on their goals for your organization. In short, get on their wavelength.

14. Remain a leader and decision maker. Don't let preoccupation with playing it safe cause you to abdicate.

Instead of letting all the confusion cause you to drift to the sidelines, wield your authority. You probably need to manage more, not less. And since mergers typically slow response times, be sure you put forth more effort to be timely, decisive, and expeditious. Don't contribute to the slippage or loss of organization momentum.

15. Show some ownership of organization problems. Don't just project blame elsewhere and expect higher management (in your company or the new parent firm) to assume all the responsibility for correcting things. Instead of being a critic and finger pointer, strive to be part of the solution.

16. Help minimize surprises. It is the unanticipated event that generates the most stress for people.

CONCLUSION

It is worth noting here that, in both the parent company and the acquired firm, the greatest sins of postmerger management are sins of omission. In opting to do nothing in an effort to avoid doing wrong, critical mistakes are made. It is, in fact, a time for stepping forth in a proactive fashion to take charge of the situation. There are opportunities to be seized and problems that should be attacked aggressively.

It is common practice for top management in the parent company to minimize the problems that develop in the acquiring and merging of another organization. Parent company executives generally give themselves pretty good marks for the way they have handled an acquisition. In strong contrast, people in the acquired firm commonly deliver scathing indictments of the way they have been treated. It seems that practically everyone who has lived through the experience of being merged or acquired has negative feelings about it.

Whether you listen to the people who have been there or whether you study the hard statistics, it is evident that management makes many mistakes in the merger/acquisition arena. It is treacherous terrain.

The truth of the matter is that companies not being merged or acquired are mismanaged all the time, too. But employees of those firms seem to get used to it. They become inured to the aggravations and frustrations that go with the status quo. Incumbents learn how to cope: They tolerate problems, learn how to work around them, and sometimes become a part of them. They resign themselves to the situation and learn how to survive in that environment.

But mergers and acquisitions bring abrupt changes, and people take notice of what's happening. The change in ownership gets their attention, breaks them out of their mental ruts, and generates concern and consternation. Organizational and individual inertia causes them to resist the changes that mergers and acquisitions bring, and that will always be so. But let us hope that the record of management success in mergers and acquisitions improves, as there is much at stake for everyone involved.

Chapter 1

1. Arthur M. Louis, "The Bottom Line on 10 Big Mergers," *Fortune* 105 (May 3, 1982), pp. 84-89.
2. Peter F. Drucker, "The Five Rules of Successful Acquisition," *The Wall Street Journal*, October 15, 1981, p. 28.

Chapter 4

1. Charles M. Leighton and G. Robert Tod, "After the Acquisition: Continuing Challenge," *Harvard Business Review* 47 (March-April 1969), p. 94.

Chapter 5

1. Richard S. Sloma, *How to Measure Managerial Performance* (New York, Macmillan, 1980), p. 3.

Price Pritchett, Ph.D., is Chairman and CEO of Pritchett & Associates, Inc., a Dallas-based onsulting firm. Dr. Pritchett has consulted to major corporations worldwide for over two decades, and is considered one of the foremost experts on merger integration strategy, business transformation, and culture change. He wrote the first edition of *After the Merger,* and has written over 20 books on individual and organizational performance.

Donald Robinson, a Manager in Pritchett & Associates' Consulting Group, has led merger integration projects in England, France, Germany, Holland, Sweden, Canada, and the United States. Robinson has published articles and been quoted in *The Journal of Mergers and Acquisitions, HR Magazine,* and *CIO.*

Russell Clarkson, Consulting Principal at Pritchett & Associates, has led the implementation of clients' merger integration and project management initiatives in support of process and organizational redesign. Clarkson has taught at Renesselaer Polytechnic Institute, and served as Director to New York University's Management Decision Laboratory.